c

||||||||||||||||||||||||||||||||
D0996722

GREY MAGIC

THE ENIGMA OF THE GREY THOROUGHBRED

CONTENTS

AUTHOR'S ACKNOWLEDGEMENTS

It is one thing to wake up in the middle of the night and think what a good idea it would be to write a book about grey Thoroughbreds, but it is quite another to compile such a book in the cold light of day; and then there is the problem of convincing a publisher that this is, at least, an essential work of reference!

When the concept of *Grey Magic* was first mooted to friends and colleagues, the reaction overall was encouraging, but it was by no means a unanimous vote of confidence. Indeed, in the car park at Newbury racecourse one day, a leading trainer said that in all honesty he could not imagine anyone wanting to read a book devoted to grey horses!

Grateful thanks are due to a number of people who did lend encouragement, however, and were happy to be associated with *Grey Magic*. First and foremost is Kirsten Rausing of Lanwades Stud, Newmarket, who kindly agreed to write the foreword; of all the Thoroughbred breeders in the UK, she probably has more reason than almost anyone to be grateful for greys.

A special word of thanks is also due to Tony Morris, Nick Wingfield Digby, MRCVS, and Patrick Brain for their particular knowledge and expertise. Many other people kindly provided information about individual horses, and none more so than Pat and Hugh McCalmont concerning The Tetrarch; Sir Michael Oswald, with his involvement at Egerton and the Royal Studs; and Julie Cecil regarding celebrated greys trained by her late father, Sir Noel Murless.

Published sources most consulted were *The Racing Calendar, The General Stud Book, Raceform, Chaseform, Racehorses* (annual Timeform publications), *The Bloodstock Breeders' Annual Review,* the *Biographical Encyclopaedia of Flat Racing,* the *Encyclopaedia of Steeplechasing, Three Centuries of Leading Sires,* the *Racing Post,* and all the leading racing and breeding periodicals, past and present.

I am also much indebted to Anne O'Connor of the Irish Thoroughbred Breeders' Association for putting me in touch with Guy St. Williams, who, together with Tony Sweeney, provided much of the detail concerning Master Robert.

Finally I would also like to thank Sue Cameron for her expertise at proof reading, Nina Clark, who demonstrated great patience and stamina when typing the original charts, Amanda Bentley of Eclipse Pedigrees at Weatherbys, together with all the production staff at Highdown, including Julian Brown and Tracey Scarlett. All of them gave invaluable assistance for which I am extremely grateful.

FOREWORD

'All cats are grey in the dark.' This piece of received wisdom can be pragmatically applied to almost anything, from Maoist politics to horse racing. The fact that a Thoroughbred racehorse happens to be grey in no way affects his or her athletic ability.

All the same through the centuries man has been fascinated by horses in general, by the evolving Thoroughbred racehorse in particular, and perhaps especially so by the greys amongst these noble animals.

In my own case, I have been fortunate enough to breed a number of good grey racehorses – indeed, my very first winner in the British Isles was Ayah, the second highest rated two-year-old filly in Ireland in 1975. More Group successes have followed with the greys Kala Dancer, European champion juvenile; Last Second; and world champion three-year-old filly, Alborada, and 2004 German Horse-of-the-Year, Albanova, two full sisters to race in my colours.

Racing aficionados frequently ask me if I set out to breed greys, but I must admit that such is not the case. Amongst the best horses I have bred have been the bays Petoski, Gateman, Rose of Zollern, Alleluia and Songerie, and the chesnut, Foreign Affairs.

Still, I naturally share the general enthusiasm for all those magnificent grey runners, past and present. It will be a long time before I forget the sight of a lovely grey filly emerging from the morning mist on top of Newmarket's Warren Hill, only a mile from where she was foaled. Even then, in March 1997, there was something special about this unraced two-year-old – she was Alborada.

In *Grey Magic*, Alan Yuill Walker sets out the parameters for the transmission of the grey colour gene in the Thoroughbred. He then goes on to record the background of numerous famous greys to have raced in Great Britain and Ireland, from Abelia to Young Emperor. His encyclopaedic knowledge of racing history certainly makes fascinating reading.

It is indeed astonishing that the grey coat of today's Thoroughbred hinges on the survival of just one stallion, Master Robert, and of the inordinate contribution made to that phenomenon by the subfertile The Tetrarch.

I thoroughly recommend this book to all lovers of the Thoroughbred, in all its many hues.

Kirsten Rausing
Lanwades Stud
Newmarket

PREFACE

The reason for writing *Grey Magic* is that grey racehorses have a unique appeal and my own fascination was compounded on discovering that all grey Thoroughbreds of the present day can trace their colour back to Master Robert, an Irish-based stallion foaled in the early part of the 19th century - a fact that will be a revelation to most breeders and racegoers alike.

My earliest appreciation of greys, however, was not owed to anything quite so erudite, but to the eminently more important pursuit of backing winners. In this respect two greys with whom Hampshire trainer, Bill Wightman, was closely involved, played a leading part. Both date back to a couple of years I spent ostensibly at the Royal Agricultural College, Cirencester, when attendance at lectures was rather more spasmodic than on the racecourse.

In June 1962 I was racing at Brighton when my future brother-in-law, a serious punter, found himself having an unsuccessful afternoon with the bookmakers. To his enquiry 'what are you backing in the next', I suggested Grey Seas, trained by Bill Wightman. As luck would have it the favourite got badly interfered with at the start and Grey Seas made all the running and held on by a neck. A serious deficit was transformed into an appreciable credit.

Then in April 1964, a two-year-old named Turret, bred by Bill Wightman and owned by the Duke of Norfolk, who had finished third on his début at Kempton a couple weeks previously, reappeared at the now defunct Alexandra Park racecourse. As an impoverished student I had the temerity to place a wager of £110 to £100 at odds on (the biggest bet of my entire life) and the obliging Turret scooted round the frying pan that was Ally Pally to score by a convincing six lengths.

The ninety-four horses featured in *Grey Magic* are by no means a definitive collection, albeit they do include all twenty of the individual grey classic winners in England during the 20th century; Tagalie, Airborne and Petite Etoile are the only dual winners. Otherwise the selection is arbitrary, but with greater emphasis placed on the better-known horses, both flat and jumping, since World War II - and the only greys trained abroad to be included are those who won classic races here.

The grey line of inheritance for all these illustrious horses is illustrated by the genealogy charts A to F. Some of those featured have been included for no better reason than that they are particular favourites. The Callant, for example, does not rank as a great horse in the general scheme of things, although anyone involved with hunter-chasers at that time might beg to differ! Also the mares, Canton Silk, Castle Moon, Jojo, Pelting and Sunbittern, are included for their marked contribution at stud and not on the racecourse.

Bearing in mind the relatively small percentage of racehorses that are grey, it is evident that, as a group, they have made a disproportionately valuable contribution, epitomised in modern times by the gallant Desert Orchid, the greatest crowd puller on the racecourse since the immortal Arkle.

Grey Magic is an endeavour to chronicle the exploits and the background to some of the other celebrated greys to have graced the Turf. Incidentally, for every one featured, the headings incorporate the owner, trainer, jockey and breeder - so far as the owner, trainer and jockey are concerned, they refer to those associated with the horse at the time of his or her most important victories.

The one name that dominates is Lester Piggott, who was involved with no fewer than fourteen of these grey stars. This is extraordinary considering that the overall total comprises a significant number of historical names, not to mention those under National Hunt Rules. And long before the advent of lady jockeys, his wife, Susan, won the Newmarket Town Plate, one of the oldest races in existence, on a grey!

On a bright sunny day, be it at Ascot in June or Cheltenham in March, there is no more magical sight as the sun's rays shaft through the elegant flowing tail of any grey in the field - poetry in motion.

Alan Yuill Walker
Kintbury

INTRODUCTION

White horses have been with us since time immemorial in religion, mythology and history. In The Bible, the Book of Revelations reveals, 'And I saw Heaven opened, and behold a white horse.' Christianity is not alone. The prophet Mohammed's horse, Borak, was a 'milk-white steed with wings of an angel, a human face and horse's cheeks'.

White horses continue to be regarded as sacred animals to many followers of the Muslim faith. As grey Arab horses are indigenous to the Middle East, inevitably they have a marked significance in that part of the world. At the funeral of King Hussein of Jordan (father-in-law of Sheikh Mohammed), his grey Arab followed the coffin with his master's riding boots reversed symbolically in their stirrups.

It was the mating of an Arab with a native Welsh pony that produced the oldest known horse in the world, a fact verified by *Guinness World Records*. In 2004 Badger, a grey standing 14.1 hands and resident at the Veteran Horse Society's centre at Cardigan in Pembrokeshire, attained the venerable age of fifty-one, which equates to 150 or more in human terms.

Nothing seems more evocative than the grey cavalry horses of old – in the Crimea there were the Scots' Greys, whose gallantry was depicted so effectively in Elisabeth Butler's painting, 'Scotland For Ever'. At Waterloo, Napoleon was mounted on Marengo, one of his favourite grey or white Arabs. His army's distinctive light grey cavalry horses originated from the Camargues, the salt marshlands of France's Rhone delta. Camargues are a resilient breed – they featured in Roman circuses and were utilised in the construction of the Suez Canal.

In one of the final offensives of World War 1, New Zealander, Bernard Freyberg, one of the most decorated of British generals, commanded his troops in action on a grey ("an ugly white German one"), until the wretched horse was killed under him; and when Douglas Gray of Skinner's Horse won the 1934 Kadir Cup, the Blue Riband of pig sticking, he shared the honours with his grey charger, Granite.

Horses have an altogether more sympathetic role to play in the modern army on ceremonial occasions – traditionally the climax of the annual passing out parade for officer cadets at the Royal Military Academy, Sandhurst, is when the adjutant rides his grey charger up the steps and disappears from view.

The unique pageantry of Royal Ascot would never be the same without the Windsor Greys in all their splendour as they head the Royal Procession up the course; and at the beginning of the 19th century when the then Prince of Wales (later George IV) went racing at Brighton, he would make his way up Race Hill in a barouche drawn by three pairs of greys.

Then there are the grey Lipizzaners of the world famous Spanish Riding School stabled in the magnificent Schönbrunn Palace in Vienna. And back home, what more picturesque sight could be imagined on the streets of London than a pair of Whitbread's dapple-grey dray horses? – when not delivering beer they were pulling the ceremonial coach at the annual Lord Mayor's Show.

Greys have always played their part in the world of entertainment and they were part and parcel of the great circuses of old, Chipperfields' and Bertram Mills'. But for sheer novelty Princess Trixie took some beating. This dapple grey from America and her owner-trainer, Harrison Barnes, enthralled audiences at the Palace Theatre in London with her ability to add and subtract and differentiate between colours – and all attempts to discredit the act failed ignominiously.

Of course, the success of greys in open competition is no means confined to racing witness the worlds of showjumping and three-day eventing. Pat Smythe's Tosca and John Whitaker's Milton are just two celebrated greys in the international showjumping arena and Ian Stark's Glenburnie and Murphy Himself are a pair of comparable grey eventers.

Surely there has never been a more controversial award in the history of equestrian sports at the Olympic Games than the individual three-day event gold medal in Athens in 2004 when Bettina Hoy and Ringwood Cockatoo of Germany were disqualified in favour of Leslie Law and Shear L'Eau representing Great Britain. But in one respect the result was unaffected – both horses were greys!

Sporting art is another genre in which grey horses have had a field day. Although the prices paid for sporting pictures do not compare to the huge sums expended on paintings by the great classical masters, they can still be considerable – at Sothebys in 2000 George Stubbs' rediscovered painting of the dapple-grey racehorse, Euston, realised £2.8m.

Another of George Stubbs' commissions was to paint Gimcrack for Lord Bolinbroke, one of the colt's six owners during his racing career. Gimcrack has a little known claim to fame – when the Republic of Panama issued a unique sheet of six miniature stamps in 1968 devoted to equine artists, one of them depicted a Stubbs' painting of the celebrated eighteenth century grey.

Perhaps the most enduring testament to this striking coat colour are the numerous white horses cut into the chalk hillsides in the southern half of England. The only one of medieval origin is the White Horse at Uffington, near Wantage, commemorating one of King Alfred's greatest victories. Significantly this particular white horse is on an escarpment of the downs just beyond the training centre of Lambourn. Local legend has it that on a flat-topped knoll below St. George slayed the dragon – on a white horse of course.

THE RACING
BACKGROUND

It is Saturday, August 16, 2003, an historic day in the annals of the Turf. The first ever race in Great Britain confined to greys is being staged on the July Course at Newmarket, the headquarters of racing – and the Grey Horse Handicap over 6 furlongs is won by the favourite, Smart Predator, from a dozen opponents.

A one-off, which will never have the ramifications of another innovative event at Newmarket, the Chesterfield Stakes, run over the same course in July 1965, the first race in Britain to be started from stalls, its undoubted popularity does go to show that greys have a tremendous following for whatever reason.

Britain was the last major racing country to adopt starting stalls and there had been races exclusive to greys before, most notably in the USA, Australasia and South Africa, but such was the success of the Newmarket version that the authorities immediately intimated that this was likely to become an annual feature and so far it has proved extremely popular.

For some inexplicable reason the public identify with grey racehorses in a unique way – take two horses of comparable ability and, should one be grey, he or she will receive all the plaudits. Quite apart from the obvious fact that they are more readily visible in a race, unless it is a foggy winter's afternoon or a sea fret engulfs Brighton racecourse, they seem to have a unique fascination.

Statistics produced by Weatherbys, publishers of the *General Stud Book* which records the progeny of all British and Irish-based Thoroughbred mares, indicate that between four and six per cent of the Thoroughbred population at any one time are greys with only blacks, a contrastingly unpopular colour (such is the stigma associated with them that they are frequently registered as brown), as very much the minority group.

Horses themselves seem to be aware of the colour factor too and some Thoroughbred stallions have a distinct aversion to covering grey mares. According to his breeder, John Hislop, the mighty Brigadier Gerard had a marked aversion to greys of both sexes.

During the 20th century twenty-three of the five English classic races were won by greys:

The One Thousand Guineas
Tagalie (1912), Taj Mah (1929), Camarée (1950), Petite Etoile (1959), Abermaid (1962), Hula Dancer (1963), Humble Duty (1970), Nocturnal Spree (1975), Shadayid (1991).

The Two Thousand Guineas
Tetratema (1920), Mr. Jinks (1929), Palestine (1950), Mystiko (1991).

The Derby
Tagalie (1912), Mahmoud (1936), Airborne (1946).

The Oaks
Sun Cap (1954), Petite Etoile (1959), Sleeping Partner (1969).

The St Leger
Caligula (1920), Airborne (1946), Bruni (1975), Silver Patriarch (1997).

The contribution made by greys during the second half of the 20th century is truly remarkable. Noel Murless, one of the great classic trainers of that period, was on record as saying, "I had four champions in my time, Abernant, Crepello, Petite Etoile and Gordon." Gordon Richards was his stable jockey (knighted, like Noel, for his services to racing), while both Abernant and Petite Etoile were greys.

In their authoritative book, *A Century of Champions*, joint authors, Tony Morris and John Randall, nominated Abernant as the top British/Irish sprinter with two more greys, Tetratema and Right Boy, in the first half dozen. Tetratema and his sire, The Tetrarch, are the only greys ever to be champion sire in the 20th century.

As a stallion, The Tetrarch stands supreme despite the fact that he suffered from infertility throughout his stallion life and about three-quarters of the horses featured in *Grey Magic* have The Tetrarch as an essential link in the thin grey line of inheritance and that reflects an overall trend. Conversely the most influential grey mare has been The Tetrarch's daughter, Mumtaz Mahal – on a wider front, she and her descendants formulated an Aga Khan classic dynasty that has been without equal.

If any one breeder has made an inordinate contribution to *Grey Magic* it has to be the present Aga Khan (Karim, Aga Khan IV) together with his father, Prince Aly Khan and his grandfather, Aga Khan III. Between them they bred Daylami, Mahmoud, Migoli, Palariva, Palestine, Petite Etoile and Taj Mah; also the dams of Abernant, Habat and Proclamation, and the grandam of Alborada and Albanova.

It is an on-going phenomenon, witness Daylami's very close grey relative, Dalakhani, the 2003 Prix de l'Arc de Triomphe hero: he does not feature in the book as the French-trained colt never won in Great Britain or Ireland.

Daylami, sire of the 2004 Irish Derby hero, Grey Swallow, with his first crop, earned most kudos racing for Sheikh Mohammed's Godolphin organisation which takes its name from the Godolphin Arabian, one of the three imported 'Arabian' stallions from whom all Thoroughbreds descend in the male line. It is another of this trio of founder stallions, the Darley Arabian, who lends his name to Sheikh Mohammed's overall bloodstock breeding operation centred on his Dalham Hall Stud.

Surprisingly greys have not featured prominently amongst the coterie of top Arab owners, albeit Sheikh Mohammed and Godolphin can claim four *Grey Magic* celebrities in Alydaress, Daylami, Indian Skimmer and Kribensis; Proclamation too comes under the same umbrella. However, the ruling family of Dubai certainly do not have the marked prejudice that Prince Khalid Abdullah from Saudi Arabia has against greys – seldom, if ever, do they feature on the Juddmonte Farms' agenda.

Greys, just like other horses, come in a multitude of guises, and be they colts or fillies, they exhibit no marked preference for any particular distance. They are just as likely to be sprinters, or middle distance performers, or stayers. In the immediate post-war period none was more popular than Sir Winston Churchill's Colonist II, whose courage and tenacity seemed to be a mirror image of his owner.

Colonist was certainly one of the most popular greys of his era, but more recently there has been a surfeit of new names, with a particularly strong representation during the 1990s. One of the stars during that period was Further Flight. He returned to a tumultuous reception after the 1995 Jockey Club Cup, when becoming the first horse to win the same Group race five times.

But perhaps the biggest impact has come in the field of National Hunt racing and no horse has caught the public imagination more in recent times than Desert Orchid – Dessiemania predated Henmania in the sporting vocabulary. A veritable icon of the winter game, he was champion steeplechaser five consecutive times when he won the King George VI 'Chase a record four times and in 1989 he became the only grey ever to win the Cheltenham Gold Cup.

There is something seasonal about a grey winner at Kempton Park on Boxing Day and Desert Orchid's quartet of 'King George' victories was to be followed by two more greys in One Man, who scored in the 1995 and 1996 renewals, and Teeton Mill in 1998. Sadly their careers ended prematurely – One Man met with a fatal accident and Teeton Mill suffered a serious leg injury. Then there were Stalbridge Colonist and Flying Wild, two of very few 'chasers ever to beat the mighty Arkle, albeit with an enormous weight advantage.

Over the winter of 2004/05 the *Racing Post* conducted a survey amongst its readers to determine their one hundred all-time favourite racehorses and no fewer than 954 individuals were nominated. The top 100 of this 'Ultimate Poll' included six greys; in reverse order they comprised Petite Etoile, Rooster Booster, Further Flight, Daylami, One Man and Desert Orchid.

One Man and Desert Orchid both made the last half dozen. In the final analysis Arkle just prevailed over Desert Orchid and between them they accounted for forty-one per cent of the vote. With Red Rum in third place, steeplechasers filled the first three places.

Rooster Booster (2003) is one of three greys to have won the Champion Hurdle since the war along with Anzio (1962) and Kribensis (1990). To quote from a report in the *Racing Post* on that inaugural Grey Horse Handicap at Newmarket: "The real grey star of the show may have been the classy Kribensis, as the former champion hurdler led the thirteen runners around the paddock before the race."

The phenomenon of grey super stars is not unique to Great Britain or Ireland and there have been such champions across the world. The two greatest greys trained anywhere are probably Spectacular Bid and Native Dancer, both of them champions in all three seasons in which they ran in the USA. Native Dancer sired the grey, Hula Dancer, winner of the 1963 One Thousand Guineas.

On average fifty per cent of a grey stallion's progeny will themselves be grey, so one eminent grey sire can exert an enormous influence in promoting the cause. Over the last few years this phenomenon has been seen in France through Linamix – in 1998 his son, Sagamix, became only the third grey to win the Prix de l'Arc de Triomphe, since when Dalakhani has added to the tally. The large number of grey National Hunt winners during the same period has much to do with the French-bred but Irish-based stallion, Roselier.

It is reasonable to suppose that Dalakhani's breeder, the present Aga Khan, will be associated with quite a high proportion of greys over the next few years following his recent purchase of the Lagardere bloodstock empire. One of France's most successful bloodstock operations, the deal included the Haras de Val Henry, along with its celebrated grey resident, Linamix, and the Haras d'Ouilly.

Considering that greys represent such a small percentage of the Thoroughbred population, they have made, and continue to make, a remarkable impact. Genetics decree that coat colour has absolutely no bearing on a racehorse's ability, but it certainly has a relevance when it comes to the sort of popularity that borders on hero worship: as devotees of any of these grey heroes will confirm, they have a charisma all of their own.

Charisma is an indefinable quality given to few people – so far as racehorses are concerned, they too are in a minority, but it certainly helps to be grey – greys are the blondes of the equine species; they seem to have all the fun. May their magic appeal continue to enthral as it always has.

GENETICS

What exactly determines a horse's colour or more especially a horse's grey colour? Fortunately the laws of genetics are relatively straightforward on the subject. Put simplistically, every foal receives one colour gene from each parent and these determine his or her own coat colour as well as the colour of any of his or her offspring. It is a fact that if a grey gene has been transmitted the resulting foal will be grey as that is the dominant colour.

So far as other colours are concerned: if one bay or brown gene and one chesnut is involved, the foal will be either bay or brown as that colour is basically dominant and chesnut is recessive. Thus a chesnut results only where the foal receives a chesnut gene from both parents.

However, many horses carry a recessive chesnut gene which is masked by the dominant grey or bay/brown, but which is equally likely to be transmitted to the next generation. Alternatively a horse may have obtained a bay/brown gene from each of the parents, or one grey and one bay/brown, in which case he will not have any chesnut offspring at all.

As a grey must have at least one grey parent, it is possible to trace any grey back so far as records allow. Because of their genetic dominance, greys were fairly common until about the mid-1800s, but a dramatic decline ensued so that, at the turn of the century, they had become quite a rarity. One of the main reasons for this drop in numbers was the dearth of top-class grey stallions, but the situation gradually improved throughout the 20th century.

Two grey parents virtually guarantee a grey offspring, but not necessarily so. For example when the grey mare, Una (dam of the grey Palestine), was mated with the grey sire, Mahmoud, she produced the brown Mehrali, a useful Aga Khan sprinter between the wars. As there is no means of ascertaining which of any pair of grey parents has transmitted the grey gene, the charts on pages 28-34 include both possible avenues of grey lineage where they occur.

Very occasionally white horses appear in the Thoroughbred, but it is a freak of nature: they are either white dominant heterozygous (Ww) or more usually sabino white (SS). There are thought to be no more than a hundred registered in the stud books of the world, albeit they are on the increase and it is no longer the once in a lifetime occurrence that it used to be. Not surprisingly the greatest incidence of white foals has occurred in the USA, an obvious reflection on the size of the Thoroughbred population there.

In the spring of 2005 the American Jockey Club reported thirty white foals registered in its stud book, twenty-one of them recorded since 1995. The first white foal to be registered was White Beauty in 1963 at Patchen Wikes Farm and this stud in east Fayette County had another white foal, a colt named White Prince, born in 2005. The principal contributor to this phenomenon in America is the Oregon-based stallion, Airdrie Apache. Since 1999, this resident at Painted Desert Farm in Redmond has sired at least fourteen white offspring.

Two of the best known examples of white Thoroughbreds in Europe raced for Sir Charles Clore, owner of Stype Wood Stud, near Hungerford, in Berkshire. Mont Blanc II, who went to stand at Elisabeth Couturié's Haras du Mesnil in Normandy, won at Lingfield Park and on Epsom Downs as a three-year-old in 1966, and his son, White Wonder, proved a useful sprint handicapper in the late 1970s. As Mont Blanc also sired chesnuts, they were clearly sabinos (skewbalds) or pintos (piebalds).

Another phenomenon concerns what are known in the Thoroughbred world as 'Birdcatcher ticks', grey or roan flecks in the coat. Birdcatcher (also known as Irish Birdcatcher), who never ran outside his native Ireland gaining all five of his victories at the Curragh, became champion sire of 1852 and 1856 and his grandson, Stockwell, became the 'Emperor of Stallions'. Quite apart from transmitting these characteristic markings, Birdcatcher was a major influence in promoting Ireland as a producer of top quality bloodstock.

Grey is a unique characteristic. While other coat colours remain constant, grey is special in so far as foals are never grey at birth, albeit they may have a few spasmodic grey hairs, usually acquiring that hue on shedding their foal coat, which invariably turns to white with advancing years; the first manifestations of grey are frequently seen around the eyes and on the muzzle. An outstanding example of this phenomenon is Desert Orchid, who was registered in the *General Stud Book* as bay or brown.

Certainly greys present their own particular problems and their sensitive skin seems to have a predisposition to saddle and girth sores. Kirsten Rausing of Lanwades Stud, the owner-breeder of the distinguished own-sisters, Alborada and Albanova, says that greys are particularly susceptible to melanomas, a form of skin cancer, and that when buying a grey one should always make a close inspection under the mane and tail.

Leading Newmarket veterinary surgeon, Nick Wingfield Digby of Rossale & Partners, explains, "Melanomas are black nodules that grow, particularly on the perineum under the tail. They are a very slow growing, but unattractive tumour. I believe their higher incidence in grey horses is related to the fact that grey horses have black skin with a high content of black pigment called melanin."

In his book *Breeding The Racehorse*, the great Italian breeder, Federico Tesio of Ribot fame, expounded his own theory on the subject. He maintained that grey was not a coat colour in the accepted sense of the word, but a disease of the pigmentation; a disease that has no other effect except to destroy the colour elements in the coats of bays, browns, chesnuts and blacks and may be passed by a parent to its offspring.

MASTER ROBERT

Arguments will always persist as to what influence a remote ancestor can possibly have in the genetic make-up of a particular horse. Most interpretations are nothing more than probabilities and possibilities, but the grey Thoroughbred, because he or she cannot skip a generation, has a unique characteristic which demonstrates that a particular gene can be transmitted over hundreds of years.

One can trace the ancestry of all modern day grey Thoroughbreds back nearly two hundred years to Master Robert, who was foaled in 1811 by Buffer out of Spinster, by Shuffle. Reference to the genealogy charts in *Grey Magic* shows that Grey Swallow (Chart C), for example, goes back at no fewer than twenty-three generations to Master Robert, a truly remarkable phenomenon.

The grey stallion, Master Robert, was bred by John Whaley of Whaley's Lodge on the Curragh. A leading figure in Irish racing in the early part of the 19th century, he served two spells as senior steward of the Turf Club – more sensationally his brother, Thomas 'Buck' Whaley, was murdered with a shotgun by a rival for the hand of an heiress named Sarah Jenkinson.

Over the course of three seasons, Master Robert scored ten victories, the majority of them on Ireland's premier racecourse. At two years, he won on his début in September at the Curragh;

the next season three of his seven victories were recorded there, including the Curragh Stakes; at four years he scored twice more at the Curragh. So he was a useful if not spectacular racehorse with an obvious liking for the home of Irish racing.

As a stallion he was advertised in the *Irish Racing Calendar* of 1824/25 as standing at Rathmore, near Naas, in Co. Kildare: 'Good winners from few TB mares, fee 4 guineas.' He did particularly well when mated with mares by Sir Walter Raleigh, and that particular union produced Drone (1823), winner of the 1826 Madrid Handicap at the Curragh, who became champion sire in Ireland in 1834 and is the principal son of Master Robert to perpetuate the thin grey line of inheritance (see charts A – E).

Chart F shows the other branch of the family which stems from Master Robert's son, Rust (1830). Also successful in the Madrid Handicap, Rust was ridden by his owner, Tom Ferguson, when winning the Royal Whip over four miles at the Curragh. The colt also won two King's Plates at Derry and a King's Plate at Down Royal.

In the male line Master Robert goes back at four generations to the mighty Herod (1758), also known as King Herod, who was bred by William, Duke of Cumberland, at his stud in Windsor Forest and was eight times champion sire from 1777 to 1784. Herod in turn traced back at four more generations to the Byerley Turk, the first of the three founding stallions, along with the Darley Arabian and the Godolphin Arabian, from whom all Thoroughbreds trace their male ancestry.

So far as that precarious grey line of inheritance is concerned, Master Robert descends through an unbroken line of seven mares to the stallion, Crab. Bred by a Mr. Cotton in Lincolnshire in 1722, Crab was champion sire in 1748, 1749 and 1750; indeed no grey emulated him as champion sire until The Tetrarch did so in 1919.

Crab produced four separate branches, but three of them died out including the one responsible for Gimcrack, the most celebrated grey horse of his era, and Gustavus, who in 1821 became the first of only four greys to win the Derby. Not only is Gimcrack commemorated at York by the oldest established two-year-old race in existence, but also by the annual Gimcrack dinner where the owner of the winner is obliged to make (or find someone else to make) a thought provoking speech.

Crab in turn inherited his grey coat from his sire, who is generally referred to as the Alcock Arabian (1704) or Alcock's Arabian. For the years 1721 and 1728, he is recorded as the first ever leading sire. However, at this point one is entering into the realms of uncertainty and speculation as different historical references come up with conflicting views.

As Michael Church points out in his admirable book, *Three Centuries of Leading Sires*, it was the custom in those days to change a horse's name with every change of ownership, and he suggests that Alcock's Arabian probably went under a wide variety of other names, including Akaster Turk, Ancaster Arabian, Brownlow Turk, Holderness Turk, Honeywood Arabian, Pelham's Grey Arabian, Sutton Arabian, Turner's Turk and William's Turk, but no one can be sure.

However, the consensus does seem to be that Alcock's Arabian was imported via Constantinople by Sir Robert Sutton and that from 1722 he became the property of the 2nd Duke of Ancaster, the same person who owned Herod's sire, Tartar. It is interesting to compare his date of foaling with that famous trio of founder stallions, the Byerley Turk (c. 1684), the Darley Arabian (1700) and the Godolphin Arabian (1724).

Herod, who exerted such an enormous influence in the USA and France through Diomed and Tourbillon respectively, was out of the mare, Cypron, bred by Sir William St. Quintin at his Scampston Stud, near the training centre of Malton in north Yorkshire. There is a fascinating modern day link here as one of William's descendants, Sir Charles Legard, Bart, lives at Scampston where his wife, Caroline, bred a top contemporary sprinter in Somnus.

Whereas the male line of Herod, with its predisposition towards breaking blood-vessels, gradually lost ground behind the omnipotent Darley Arabian strain, it has retained a unique standing so far as the Thoroughbred species is concerned through Master Robert – but for him it is doubtful that there would be any greys on the racecourse today. Somewhat ironically a gelding of the same name won the 1924 Grand National.

GREYS FEATURED

ABELIA	DESERT ORCHID
ABERMAID	DRAGONARA PALACE
ABERNANT	ENVIRONMENT FRIEND
ABSALOM	ERIMO HAWK
AIRBORNE	FLYING WILD
ALBANOVA	FURTHER FLIGHT
ALBORADA	GREY ABBEY
ALTHREY DON	GREY SOVEREIGN
ALYDARESS	GREY SWALLOW
ANZIO	HABAT
BARON BLAKENEY	HULA DANCER
BIRDBROOK	HUMBLE DUTY
BRUNI	INDIAN SKIMMER
CALIGULA	IRIS'S GIFT
CALL EQUINAME	JOJO
CAMAREE	KALAGLOW
CANTON SILK	KRIBENSIS
CASSANDRA GO	MAHMOUD
CASTLE MOON	MIGOLI
CATERINA	MR. JINKS
COLONIST II	MUMTAZ MAHAL
CRY OF TRUTH	MYROBELLA
DAYLAMI	MYSTIKO

NICER
NICOLAUS SILVER
NOCTURNAL SPREE
ONE MAN
PALARIVA
PALESTINE
PASTY
PELTING
PETITE ETOILE
PETONG
PORTLAW
PRECIPICE WOOD
PROCLAMATION
QUORUM
RAFFINGORA
RIGHT BOY
ROAN ROCKET
ROOSTER BOOSTER
ROYAL MINSTREL
RUBY TIGER
RUNNYMEDE
SARITAMER
SECRET STEP
SHADAYID

SHARP EDGE
SILKEN GLIDER
SILVER PATRIARCH
SLEEPING PARTNER
SOVEREIGN PATH
STALBRIDGE COLONIST
SUN CAP
SUNBITTERN
SUNY BAY
SUPREME SOVEREIGN
TAGALIE
TAG END
TAJ MAH
TEETON MILL
TERIMON
TETRATEMA
THE CALLANT
THE TETRARCH
TOWN CRIER
VIGO
VILMORIN
WARPATH
WHAT'S UP BOYS
YOUNG EMPEROR

GENEALOGY CHARTS

The following charts show how all ninety-four greys featured in this book (these are in bold type, the males in capitals) trace their grey coat colour back to Master Robert who was foaled in 1811.

Just a handful have not one, but two grey parents and, as it is impossible to ascertain which of the pair transmitted the grey gene, both independent lines are included.

A further concentration arises with the Aga Khan-bred stallions, Zeddaan and his son, Kalamoun. Because each of these two greys have two grey parents, they provide not two, but three possible sources for the grey line of inheritance – through their sires and through their respective dams, Vareta and Khairunissa.

This scenario also applies to the grey own-sisters, Alborada and Albanova as their grandam, Alruccaba, has two grey parents, with Zeddaan as her maternal grandsire.

CHART A

MASTER ROBERT

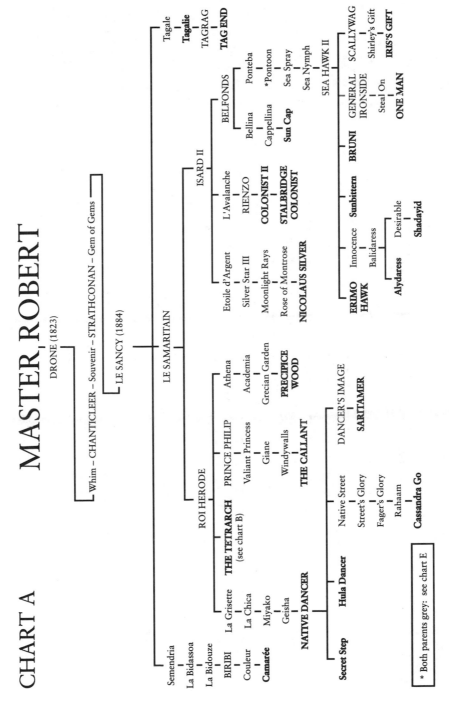

DRONE (1823)

Whim – CHANTICLEER – Souvenir – STRATHCONAN – Gem of Gems

LE SANCY (1884)

LE SAMARITAIN

ISARD II

Tagale
Tagalie
TAGRAG
TAG END

BELFONDS

Bellina
Cappellina
Sun Cap

Ponteba
*Pontoon
Sea Spray
Sea Nymph

SEA HAWK II

SCALLYWAG
Shirley's Gift
IRIS'S GIFT

L'Avalanche
RIENZO
COLONIST II
STALBRIDGE COLONIST

BRUNI

GENERAL IRONSIDE
Steal On
ONE MAN

Etoile d'Argent
Silver Star III
Moonlight Rays
Rose of Montrose
NICOLAUS SILVER

Sunbittern

Innocence
Balidaress
Desirable
Shadayid

ERIMO HAWK

Alydaress

ROI HERODE

THE TETRARCH
(see chart B)

PRINCE PHILIP
Valiant Princess

Giane
Windywalls

THE GALLANT

Athena
Academia
Grecian Garden
PRECIPICE WOOD

DANCER'S IMAGE

SARITAMER

Semendria
La Bidassoa
La Bidouze

BIRIBI
La Grisette
Couleur
La Chica
Miyako
Camarée
Geisha

NATIVE DANCER

Hula Dancer

Secret Step

Native Street
Street's Glory
Fager's Glory
Rahaam
Cassandra Go

* Both parents grey: see chart E

29

CHART B

MASTER ROBERT

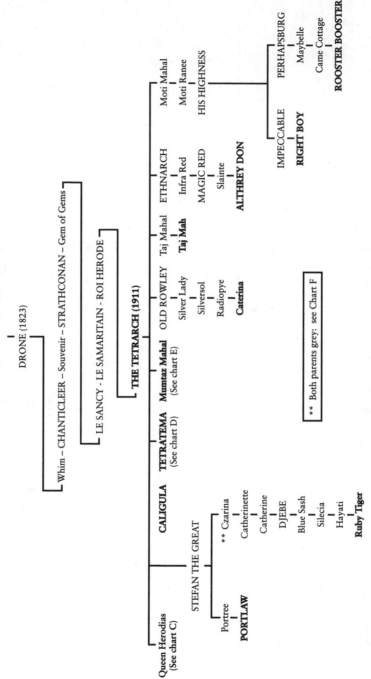

DRONE (1823)

Whim – CHANTICLEER – Souvenir – STRATHCONAN – Gem of Gems

LE SANCY - LE SAMARITAIN - ROI HERODE

THE TETRARCH (1911)

Queen Herodias
(See chart C)

CALIGULA

TETRATEMA
(See chart D)

Mumtaz Mahal
(See chart E)

OLD ROWLEY

Silver Lady

Silversol

Radiopye

Caterina

Taj Mahal

Taj Mah

ETHNARCH

Infra Red

MAGIC RED

Slainte

ALTHREY DON

Moti Mahal

Moti Ranee

HIS HIGHNESS

PERHAPSBURG

Maybelle

Came Cottage

ROOSTER BOOSTER

IMPECCABLE

RIGHT BOY

STEFAN THE GREAT

Portree

PORTLAW

** Czarina

Catherinette

Catherine

DJEBE

Blue Sash

Silecia

Hayati

Ruby Tiger

** Both parents grey: see Chart F

CHART C

MASTER ROBERT

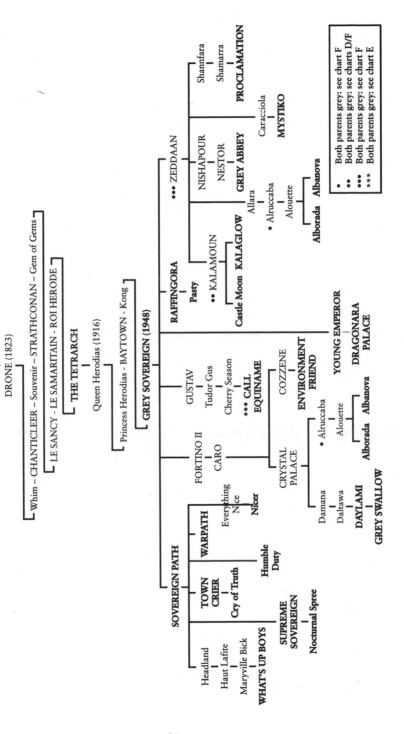

DRONE (1823)

Whim – CHANTICLEER – Souvenir – STRATHCONAN – Gem of Gems

LE SANCY - LE SAMARITAIN - ROI HERODE

THE TETRARCH

Queen Herodias (1916)

Princess Herodias - BAYTOWN - Kong

GREY SOVEREIGN (1948)

SOVEREIGN PATH

Headland
Haut Lafite
Maryville Bick
WHAT'S UP BOYS

SUPREME SOVEREIGN
Nocturnal Spree

TOWN CRIER
Cry of Truth

Humble Duty

WARPATH
Everything Nice
Nicer

FORTINO II
CARO

GUSTAV
Tudor Gus
Cherry Season
*** CALL EQUINAME

CRYSTAL PALACE

Damana
Daltawa
DAYLAMI
GREY SWALLOW

• Alruccaba
Alouette
Alborada **Albanova**

COZZENE

ENVIRONMENT FRIEND

YOUNG EMPEROR
DRAGONARA PALACE

RAFFINGORA
Pasty

•• KALAMOUN
Castle Moon **KALAGLOW**

••• ZEDDAAN

NISHAPOUR
NESTOR
GREY ABBEY

Caracciola
MYSTIKO

Shannfara
Shamarra
PROCLAMATION

Allara
• Alruccaba
Alouette
Alborada **Albanova**

• Both parents grey: see chart F
•• Both parents grey: see charts D/F
••• Both parents grey: see chart F
*** Both parents grey: see chart E

31

CHART D

MASTER ROBERT

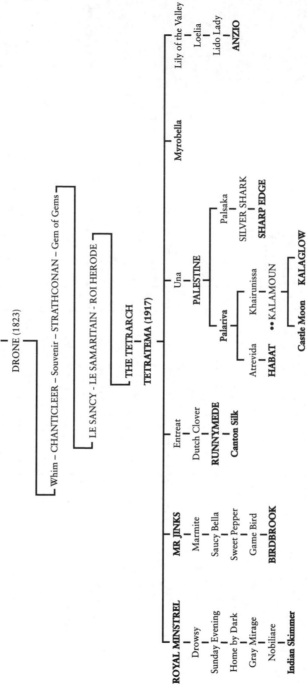

DRONE (1823)

Whim – CHANTICLEER – Souvenir – STRATHCONAN – Gem of Gems

LE SANCY · LE SAMARITAIN · ROI HERODE

THE TETRARCH
TETRATEMA (1917)

Una

PALESTINE

Palsaka

SILVER SHARK

SHARP EDGE

Myrobella

Lily of the Valley

Loelia

Lido Lady

ANZIO

Palariva

Khairunissa

••KALAMOUN

Castle Moon   **KALAGLOW**

Atrevida

HABAT

Entreat

Dutch Clover

RUNNYMEDE

Canton Silk

MR JINKS

Marmite

Saucy Bella

Sweet Pepper

Game Bird

BIRDBROOK

ROYAL MINSTREL

Drowsy

Sunday Evening

Home by Dark

Gray Mirage

Nobiliare

Indian Skimmer

•• Both parents grey: see charts C/F

DRONE (1823)

Whim – CHANTICLEER – Souvenir – STRATHCONAN – Gem of Gems

LE SANCY - LE SAMARITAIN - ROI HERODE

THE TETRARCH

Mumtaz Mahal (1921)

Rustom Mahal

Mah Mahal

Mah Iran

MAHMOUD

Polamia
GREY DAWN II
Early Rising
SILVER PATRIARCH

Star Sapphire
Tula Gorm
Tula Melody
Iridium
ROSELIER
PETONG

Stone of Fortune
FASTNET ROCK
Peace Rose
SUNY BAY

Old Dutch
Sleeping Partner

Faramoude
Farandole II
ROAN ROCKET
Rosy Morn
Nicholas Grey
TERIMON

* Pontoon
Sea Spray
Sea Nymph
SEA HAWK II

SCALLYWAG
Shirley's Gift
IRIS'S GIFT

GENERAL IRONSIDE
Steal On
ONE MAN

Innocence
Balidaress
BRUNI
Sunbittern
ERIMO HAWK

Desirable
Shadayid
Alydaress

MIGOLI
Star of Iran
Petite Etoile

Abelia
Chysanthia
Teleflora

Abracadabra
Belle de Retz
Aquaria

Sea Imp
Abermaid

ABWAH
ABSALOM

ABERNANT

BELFORT **KRIBENSIS**
BARON
BLAKENEY **EQUINAME**
***CALL

*	Both parents grey: see chart A
***	Both parents grey: see chart C

CHART F

MASTER ROBERT

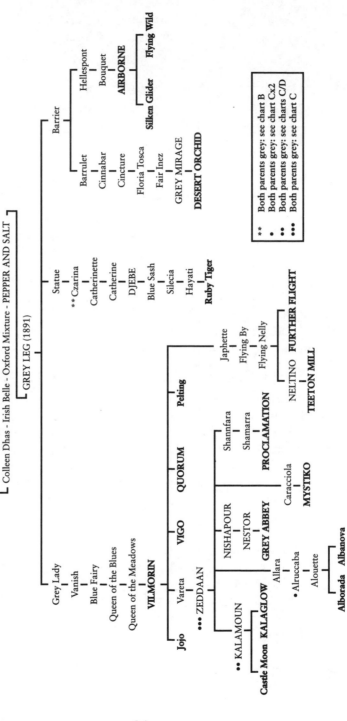

RUST (1830)

Colleen Dhas - Irish Belle - Oxford Mixture - PEPPER AND SALT

GREY LEG (1891)

Barrier
Hellespont
Bouquet
AIRBORNE
Silken Glider   **Flying Wild**

Barrulet
Cinnabar
Cincture
Floria Tosca
Fair Inez
GREY MIRAGE
DESERT ORCHID

Statue
** Czarina
Catherinette
Catherine
DJEBE
Blue Sash
Silecia
Hayati
Ruby Tiger

Grey Lady
Vanish
Blue Fairy
Queen of the Blues
Queen of the Meadows
VILMORIN

Pelting

Japhette
Flying By
Flying Nelly   **FURTHER FLIGHT**
NELTINO   **TEETON MILL**

QUORUM

Shannfara
Shamarra
PROCLAMATION

VIGO

Caracciola
MYSTIKO

Vareta
••• ZEDDAAN

NISHAPOUR
NESTOR
GREY ABBEY

Jojo

•• KALAMOUN
Castle Moon KALAGLOW

Allara
• Alruccaba
Alouette
Alborada Albanova

Albanova

Both parents grey: see chart B   **
Both parents grey: see chart Cx2   •
Both parents grey: see charts C/D   ••
Both parents grey: see chart C   •••

34

ABELIA

Grey, 1955, by Abernant - Queen of Peru

Owner: Bernard Hornung
Trainer: Sir Noel Murless
Jockey: Lester Piggott
Breeder: West Grinstead Stud Ltd.

As many of his patrons were leading owner-breeders, like the Sassoons and the Joels, Noel Murless invariably advised them over their studs and inevitably they supported many of the leading horses he had trained, both at Beckhampton and at Warren Place, as stallions.

Another owner was Bernard Hornung, whose breeding operation was labelled West Grinstead Stud Ltd, near Horsham. After his father died in 1940, he had sold the stud where the Derby winner, Papyrus, stood, establishing a smaller enterprise at his home, High Hurst Manor, close by at Cowfold. Meanwhile the West Grinstead premises became in turn an annexe for the National Stud and then the Sussex Stud.

Bernard Hornung's favourite was Abelia. She had inherited the grey coat of her sire, Abernant, and was held in similar esteem by Noel Murless. But she might have been supplanted in Hornung's affections by another homebred filly in Aunt Edith. An unraced two-year-old when her owner-breeder died in February 1964, she became the first of her sex to win the King George VI and Queen Elizabeth Stakes a couple of years later.

Like Aunt Edith, Abelia carried the distinctive Hornung colours of 'white, black spots and sleeves, red cap', but the two fillies could hardly have been more dissimilar in ability. Out of the gate like a flash, the Abernant filly excelled as a juvenile over 5 furlongs, winning the Queen Mary Stakes, July Stakes, Molecomb Stakes and Cornwallis Stakes, with her characteristic flashing tail.

Second in the Lowther Stakes and Cheveley Park Stakes, she beat another grey Abernant filly, Ruthin, at Goodwood, while the runner-up at the Newmarket July Meeting was The Queen's surprise Two Thousand Guineas hero, Pall Mall. From just two outings at three years, Abelia won the Alington Stakes, Sandown Park, and was a well beaten third at Royal Ascot in the King's Stand Stakes.

A noted broodmare for the home stud, two of Abelia's best offspring were the grey Never Say Die siblings, Casabianca (Royal Hunt Cup, Royal Lodge Stakes), and Sea Lavender (Fred Darling Stakes).

She also had two distinguished grey grandsons with Grey Baron (Henry II Stakes, Goodwood Cup, Jockey Club Cup), and King Midas (Cambridgeshire). Grey Baron won the Goodwood Cup in record time and proved the best horse bred by another Sussex breeder, John Walker of Sullington Stud, near Storrington. Abelia is also the fourth dam of a smart two-year-old and sire in Petardia.

During all the years that Noel Murless trained at Warren Place, his daughter, Julie Cecil, cannot recall any inmate who could whip round so quickly as Abelia. She was ridden out regularly by Spider Gibson, the long serving head lad, but she never managed to drop him. Spider is the father of leading Newmarket estate agent, Alan, also a successful bloodstock breeder, and he in turn is the father of jockey, Dale Gibson.

ABERMAID

Grey, 1959, by Abernant - Dairymaid

Owners: Sir Percy Loraine, Bart, Roderic More O'Ferrall, Lord Elveden
Trainer: Harry Wragg
Jockey: Bill Williamson
Breeders: Sir Percy Loraine, Bart, Roderic More O'Ferrall

Today Kildangan Stud, Monasterevin, Co. Kildare, is the magnificent Irish breeding headquarters of Sheikh Mohammed, but it used to be the family home of Roderic More O'Ferrall, who started a small stud there when he gave up training in the 1930s as well as planting many of the magnificent trees that add so much to its present splendour.

On 1st January 1953, Roderic, whose family name is synonymous with the world-wide advertising agency, became partners with his old friend, the former diplomat, Sir Percy Loraine, in their shared bloodstock interests – up till then they had maintained separate breeding entities albeit based at Kildangan.

One of the mares involved was Dairymaid, whose dam, Laitron, had been acquired by Percy Loraine as a barren mare for 400 guineas. In 1953 and 1954 Kildangan Stud had been responsible for the Two Thousand Guineas winners, Nearula and Darius. Dairymaid was to provide the stud with another classic success at Newmarket when her daughter, Abermaid, emulated Percy Loraine's homebred Queenpot in winning the 1962 One Thousand Guineas.

While Nearula had been sold as yearling (by then Kildangan was one of Ireland's leading commercial studs), Abermaid was retained. As a juvenile she was unbeaten in three starts culminating with the New (later Norfolk) Stakes, Royal Ascot. The intermediate of them was on the Tuesday of the York May Meeting and the next day the same Percy Loraine colours prevailed with Ambergris in the Musidora Stakes.

The following week their owner died at his London home aged eighty. So the two fillies continued to race for Roderic More O'Ferrall and his new partner, Guinness heir, Lord Elveden – Ambergris won the Irish Oaks (she had already finished second in the One Thousand Guineas and the Oaks), while Abermaid won the following season's One Thousand Guineas. Both fillies were trained by Harry Wragg.

Back home at Kildangan, Abermaid's best progeny proved to be Great Host (Great Voltigeur Stakes, Chester Vase), a son of Ambergris' sire, Sicambre. In 1968 she was exported to the USA, having been bought privately by Paul Mellon for his Rokeby Farms in Virginia through the Anglo-Irish Agency of which Roderic More O'Ferrall's brother, Frank, was a director.

Harry Wragg, known as the head waiter in his riding days for obvious reasons, also trained a second *Grey Magic* star in Supreme Sovereign, while another, Cassandra Go, was trained by son, Geoff, his successor at Abington Place.

ABERNANT

Grey, 1946, by Owen Tudor - Rustom Mahal

Owner: Sir Reginald Macdonald-Buchanan
Trainer: Sir Noel Murless
Jockey: Sir Gordon Richards
Breeder: Lady Macdonald-Buchanan

Abernant and Petite Etoile, two of the outstanding horses trained by Noel Murless, the archetypal trainer of classic winners, were grey homebred descendants of the celebrated grey Mumtaz Mahal. But whereas the latter was trained at Warren Place, the former was trained at Beckhampton, near Marlborough, in Wiltshire, before Noel moved to Newmarket.

Abernant, whom Murless always rated the fastest he ever handled, was owned by Reginald Macdonald-Buchanan and bred in Newmarket by his wife, Catherine, at her Lordship Stud on the Cambridge Road by the homebred stallion, Owen Tudor; the Gold Cup winner was then standing at the adjacent New England Stud, but later moved to her other Newmarket stud, Egerton.

Abernant's dam, Rustom Mahal, a half-sister to the respective dams of Mahmoud and Nasrullah, was bred, like them, by the Aga Khan, who sold her privately to the Macdonald-Buchanans. Evidently she showed exceptional speed on the Beckhampton gallops, but was devoid of steering or brakes – she always worked upsides between two companions to keep her straight, but for safety reasons she never set foot on a racecourse.

Sir Reginald and Lady Macdonald-Buchanan, as they became, lived at Cottesbrooke Hall, a magnificent Queen Anne house in the Pytchley country, thought to have been the inspiration for Jane Austen's Mansfield Park. As owners, both had black and white racing colours, reflecting the most famous brand of whisky of the family distillers, James Buchanan & Sons.

Every year on his annual pilgrimage for racing at Goodwood, Noel Murless would combine a visit to the Macdonald-Buchanans' nearby Lavington Stud in the lee of the Sussex Downs to inspect their yearlings, who had been transferred from Newmarket as weanlings the previous autumn.

In the summer of 1947 a group of four yearling colts was paraded for Noel and his predecessor at Beckhampton, Fred Darling. "You don't want the grey," observed Fred, "he's just a little rat." Noel remembered the occasion well. "I asked if I could see him turned out in the paddock and watch him move. Away they went and it was then that I saw that wonderful action. I said to Fred, 'We couldn't possibly leave him behind.' He agreed."

A brilliant two-year-old, he won the Chesham, Champagne and Middle Park Stakes, all by a minimum of five lengths. He suffered the narrowest of defeats in the Two Thousand Guineas by the subsequent Derby winner, Nimbus, before concentrating on sprinting, winning the July Cup, King George Stakes and Nunthorpe Stakes, victories he repeated famously as a four-year-old.

Also successful in the King's Stand Stakes at three years, he was champion in all three seasons in training and was probably the greatest sprinter of the 20th century. Noel Murless described him as "A wonderful horse, the kindest animal in the world."

Gordon Richards was just as enthusiastic in his appraisal: "A great favourite of mine, a tremendous character with a pronounced personality all his own – just like a big, faithful old dog." Comparatively speaking the great jockey rated Abernant, Myrobella and Tiffin as the fastest horses he ever rode, with Abernant as the fastest of the colts.

Julie Murless, as she then was, recalls that the grey adored children. "Regularly at stable time I used to sit on his back and I'm probably the only person alive to do so. Before he won the

Nunthorpe for the second time he was so preoccupied watching some children playing that Gordon was afraid that he'd lost his concentration. However, once he was called up, he was all racehorse."

Sir Michael Oswald, who managed Egerton Stud when Abernant stood there, remembers Gordon saying that, unlike the majority of sprinters, his propulsion came not from behind but from in front. His conformation as described by Michael bears this out. "While he did not have the best of hindlegs, his forelegs were exemplary and he had a great front end with a very powerful neck, an excellent shoulder, and a very strong forearm."

Although he had a smart grandson in Absalom, Abernant failed to establish a male line of his own and it may be significant that with his slightly effeminate head he took much more after his dam's line than that of his sire. Responsible for the winners of over a thousand races worldwide, his stud career at Egerton blossomed primarily through the efforts of his daughters, both on the racecourse and at stud. Two of them, Abermaid and Abelia, feature in *Grey Magic*, while another, Flattering, is the dam of Humble Duty.

Inadvertently, Abernant made a valuable contribution to the career of Noel Murless' other grey celebrity, as his daughter, Julie, explains. "When Petite Etoile was kept in training at five, she had to have a grey colt in front of her in the string and a grey filly behind her; she would look round and if the filly was not there, she would go mad." The obliging pair, Eddy and Dolgelley, were both three-year-olds by Abernant.

The Macdonald-Buchanans named their star after the Welsh home on the River Wye of their friend, Lord Trevethin, uncle to that sage of the Turf, Lord Oaksey. After he won at Royal Ascot as a two-year-old, Trevethin dispatched a telegram to his owner, 'Congratulations. Flag flying at Abernant'. Thereafter raising the standard was to become a poignant ritual in recognition of all his many subsequent victories.

ABSALOM

Grey, 1975, by Abwah - Shadow Queen

Owner: Anne Alington
Trainer: Ryan Jarvis
Jockeys: Lester Piggott, Taffy Thomas
Breeder: Melissa Williamson

It was coincidental that two Group winning half-brothers, Absalom and Adonijah, should have wound up on adjoining studs at Newmarket, the former at Dunchurch Lodge Stud (now called Rockingham Stud) and the latter at Someries Stud – today both are part of Sheikh Mohammed's vast domain lying between Duchess Drive and Woodditton Road.

A grey standing just 15.2 hands high, Absalom (originally registered in the *General Stud Book* as Absolom) was the last good winner trained by Ryan Jarvis, who was succeeded by his son, William, winning the Cornwallis Stakes at two years, Haydock Park Sprint Cup at three years, and Premio Chiusura and Diadem Stakes at four years. He raced for Anne Alington, vice-chairman of the British Red Cross Society.

"We were very lucky to find him in the first place," recalled Michael Wyatt of Dunchurch Lodge. "I approached Ryan Jarvis about buying him around Ascot week of his four-year-old career. Eventually I agreed to pay the partners in the horse £160,000, with the contingency of an additional £40,000 should he win another Pattern race in England or France – I've never been so pleased to write out another cheque!"

Retired to Dunchurch Lodge for the 1980 season, he replaced another grey there in Roan Rocket. Both had been yearling purchases at the Newmarket October Sales. Absalom cost 3,000 guineas when consigned from Summertree Stud at Bodle Street, near Hailsham, in East Sussex, owned by Gerrard and Melissa Williamson.

The Williamsons subsequently moved their stud to Leighton Buzzard before returning to East Sussex, but to a different location, this time at Robertsbridge. A former master of the East Sussex Hunt (which was amalgamated with the Romney Marsh), Melissa was a cousin of the well known Irish breeder, Liz Burke, mother of two key racing and breeding personalities, Sir Thomas Pilkington, former senior steward of the Jockey Club, and Sonia Rogers of Airlie Stud in Ireland.

It was close to Leighton Buzzard – at Southcourt Stud – that Absalom concluded his stallion career. One of the last surviving links in the Abernant male line, Absalom's greatest gift to posterity was to sire Dead Certain (Cheveley Park Stakes, Lowther Stakes, Queen Mary Stakes), the champion two-year-old sprint filly of 1989.

He is also the maternal grandsire of Smart Predator, the first winner of the inaugural 'greys only' race at Newmarket.

AIRBORNE

Grey, 1943, by Precipitation - Bouquet

Owner: John Ferguson
Trainer: Dick Perryman
Jockey: Tommy Lowrey
Breeder: Harold Boyd-Rochfort

Although he started at 50-1, Airborne was a popular choice with certain members and ex-members of the armed forces who converged in their droves on Epsom Downs to watch the 1946 Derby, the first Blue Riband to be staged at its traditional home since the 1939 renewal.

The grey was trained by Dick Perryman, a former number one jockey to Lord Derby, at Beaufort Cottage Stables at the top end of Newmarket High Street, now utilised by leading veterinary practice, Rossdale & Partners. Not only did he win the Derby, but he also proceeded to win the St. Leger – the precincts of Doncaster racecourse were cleared of German prisoners of war just in time for the final classic.

Unsuccessful in four starts as a juvenile, he was big and backward at that stage as Dick Perryman explained, "The main purpose of those races was to keep Airborne quiet. He was such a playful devil at exercise, though there was no harm in him. When it came to serious business he never once turned his head."

The son of Precipitation was kept in training as a four-year-old with the Gold Cup as his objective, but he developed a persistent dry cough that spring which precluded him from ever running again. He was retired to Aislabie Stud, known nowadays as Collin Stud, on the outskirts of Newmarket at Stetchworth, which his owner, John Ferguson, a plastics manufacturer from Godalming in Surrey, subsequently leased to Dick Perryman.

In the spring of 2005, a dispute arose over the inheritance of Collin Stud which resulted in litigation in the High Court. The two daughters of former trainer, Neil Adam, who suffered from multiple sclerosis, contested their father's controversial will leaving the property to two of his stud employees. The claimants won their case.

There were high hopes that Airborne would help to resurrect the flagging fortunes of the Matchem male line. In the event he proved a failure as a flat sire with the notable exception of the grey Irish Oaks winner, Silken Glider, but many of his progeny did well under National Hunt Rules. Amongst his 'chasers were Flyingbolt (Champion 'Chase, Irish Grand National), Frenchman's Cove (Whitbread Gold Cup), and Flying Wild (Massey-Ferguson Gold Cup).

A grey mare, Flying Wild was bred by Airborne's breeder, Harold Boyd-Rochfort, owner of the Middleton Park Stud, Co. Westmeath, in Ireland. He had received 3,300 guineas for Airborne as a yearling when consigned to the Newmarket September Sales.

The selection was made on John Ferguson's behalf by his then trainer, Walter Earl. It was one of his patrons, Stanhope Joel, who had persuaded his old school friend, John Ferguson, to become a racehorse owner, the latter adopting similar pink and green racing colours – the two families used to share a house together in Newmarket for race-weeks and the sales.

Airborne's sire, Precipitation, had been reared at Middleton Park on behalf of Sir Harold and Lady Zia Wernher – they were patrons of the powerful Freemason Lodge stable at Newmarket presided over by Harold's youngest brother, Cecil. It was very much a family affair, as the eldest brother, Arthur, who was killed in the war, had owned Airborne's dam, Bouquet. Furthermore, upon his retirement, his jockey, Tommy Lowrey, became an invaluable Freemason Lodge work rider.

Airborne was the fourth grey to win the Derby, following the moderate Gustavus (1821), the filly, Tagalie (1912), and the elegant Mahmoud (1936) – the latter pair both feature in *Grey Magic*.

Until 1956, Airborne stood as a syndicated stallion at Aislabie Stud. He was then sold cheaply to Robert Way of Hall Stud, Burrough Green, just down the road, better known nowadays as a livery yard run by Candy Sasse. Robert Way, the well known dealer in antiquarian racing books, was the breeder of the aforementioned star 'chaser, Flyingbolt. Finally the Derby winner was moved to Gerry Langford's Ardenrun Stud, close to Lingfield Park racecourse, where he died from heart failure in 1962, aged nineteen.

Shortly after his Derby success, John Ferguson remarked, "Most people try for years, and then unsuccessfully, to own a classic winner, yet it has come to me at the very beginning. It is almost unfair to be deprived of the long years of expectant and exasperating anticipation!"

Two years before he died in 1956, John Ferguson nearly did it again when homebred Arabian Night finished runner-up to Never Say Die at Epsom.

ALBANOVA

Grey, 1999, by Alzao - Alouette

Owner: Kirsten Rausing
Trainer: Sir Mark Prescott, Bart
Jockeys: Terry Hellier, Seb Sanders
Breeder: Kirsten Rausing

There is an understandable tendency for breeders to repeat a previously successful mating, but it is very much a case of the heart ruling the head as very few own-brothers or sisters are of comparable ability. But just occasionally replicating an already proven formula is more than justified.

No better example has been provided in recent times than by Albanova and her older sister, Alborada – the former was conceived when the latter had not long turned three years of age. The two grey fillies were bred by Kirsten Rausing of Lanwades Stud, at Moulton, on the outskirts of Newmarket, a member of the reclusive Swedish clan whose fortune accrues from international packaging giant, Tetra Pak.

As this was prior to Alborada gaining her two famous victories in the Champion Stakes, one might conclude that the mating was done without the benefit of hindsight. But that would only be partially true as previously Kirsten and her friend, Sonia Rogers, had bred to their sire, Alzao, the 1996 Nassau Stakes and Sun Chariot Stakes (both now elevated to Group 1 status) heroine, Last Second, who is out of Alruccaba, the grandam of Albanova and Alborada.

Miss Rausing acquired Alruccaba, from her breeder, the Aga Khan. She says, "I bought her at the 1985 December Sales for one bid – 19,000 guineas. The reserve was 18,000 guineas. I was amazed she didn't make more. Anyone there at the sales could have bought her."

Alruccaba, a winning two-year-old, but unsound for further racing, shares her grandam, both of whose parents were grey, with Nishapour (who became a Lanwades stallion), this being the same branch of the Mumtaz Mahal family as the famous greys, Mahmoud and Petite Etoile.

Successful in listed races at three and four years, Albanova became the very first horse that her owner-breeder kept in training as a five-year-old, and the decision was vindicated in spectacular fashion. Having completely overcome her aversion to starting stalls, she was to be unbeaten in three starts, thereby outperforming her illustrious sister by winning three Group 1 events.

This hat trick of wins in Germany comprised the Deutschland Preis at Dusseldorf in July, and two events in Cologne, the Rheinland Pokal in August and the Preis von Europa in September. The first to complete that particular treble in the same season, she is also the first filly to score in the Preis von Europa in which she had finished runner-up the previous year. In 2004 she was voted German 'Horse of the Year' when her dam, Alouette, earned the TBA's 'Broodmare of the Year' award.

Whereas Alborada gained both her Champion Stakes victories for stable jockey, George Duffield, he missed out on Albanova's German odyssey as he was hors de combat with an injured shoulder, but Terry Hellier and Seb Sanders certainly proved admirable replacements. In fact that injury terminated George Duffield's riding career and a thirty-year association with Sir Mark Prescott which must have been the longest in the business.

In November 2004, on the Sunday evening spanning Tattersalls' December Sales, Kirsten Rausing held a stallion show and dinner at her affiliated St. Simon Stud at Kennett to celebrate her quarter of a century at Lanwades as well as Albanova's unique success in Germany, when the two grey sisters were toasted by hundreds of well-wishers.

ALBORADA

Grey, 1995, by Alzao - Alouette

Owner: Kirsten Rausing
Trainer: Sir Mark Prescott, Bart
Jockey: George Duffield
Breeder: Kirsten Rausing

As Albanova precedes Alborada in alphabetical sequence, much of the relevant background information to these two distinguished own-sisters has already been mentioned in the preceding chapter, but in terms of merit this remarkable pair of greys should be regarded in reverse order.

Triptych (1986/87) and Alborada (1998/99) are the only two fillies to win the Champion Stakes twice and they are two of the only four dual winners since the war. Remarkably each filly won on both the Rowley Course and on the July Course at Newmarket – racing was transferred to the summer venue for Alborada's second victory due to the construction of the controversial Millennium Stand. Coincidentally another grey filly called Alborada distinguished herself on the July Course when winning the 1964 Falmouth Stakes.

Homebred by Kirsten Rausing at her pristine Lanwades Stud, Alborada, whom she refers to as 'the grey pearl', is out of Alouette, a grey mare bred in partnership with her close friend, Sonia Rogers of Airlie Stud in Ireland. It was from Sonia Rogers' late husband, Tim, a pioneer in stallion promotion, that Kirsten learnt the business – she had a particularly high profile as chairman of the European Federation of Thoroughbred Breeders' Associations.

The first Group 1 winner to emerge from Lanwades under Miss Rausing's management was the grey Dewhurst Stakes winner, Kala Dancer, by the resident stallion Niniski, and the latter was then joined by another grey in Nishapour – it afforded Kirsten Rausing immense satisfaction that he is the only stallion that the present Aga Khan has ever boarded in Newmarket.

But for fracturing a pedal-bone as a foal, Alborada would have gone to the yearling sales instead of carrying Kirsten Rausing's distinctive green and white colours. The filly emulated her close relative, Last Second, in winning the Park Stakes at the Curragh on her two-year-old finale, before winning the following season's Pretty Polly Stakes (Curragh), Nassau Stakes and Champion Stakes.

On her only other start at three, Alborada was a good second to the mighty Swain in the Irish Champion Stakes. However, all sorts of problems, a throat infection, a splint and corns on a foot, limited her four-year-old campaign to just two starts the ensuing season. Her repeat victory in the Champion Stakes was prefaced by a solitary run at Goodwood in July in the Nassau Stakes. Running slightly wide on the top bend, she slipped and nearly fell. "For one heart stopping moment I actually thought she had broken a leg," Kirsten recalls.

Keeping Alborada in training as a four-year-old was not quite the sporting gesture that it might suggest. Her owner-breeder had planned to have her covered for the 1999 season by Danzig, but it transpired that no nominations were available to the Claiborne Farm stallion for the next two years. Kirsten explains, "Towards the end of 1998 I was able to buy a breeding right to Danzig for 2000. In this way I was effectively acting in the long term futures' market and a nomination price was accordingly adjusted downwards."

One of the perennial problems facing breeders is the necessity to cull breeding stock from time to time and Alouette's own-sister, Jude, has proved an invaluable broodmare since being sold as a yearling. She is the dam of two Group 1 winning fillies in Ireland in Yesterday (Irish 1000 Guineas), and Irish champion two-year-old, Quarter Moon, both of whom finished runner-up in the Oaks.

At Sir Mark Prescott's historic Heath House Stables in Newmarket his predecessors are commemorated by wall plaques together with lists of the more famous horses they trained. However, Alborada (Spanish for dawn or sunrise) has her own memento – a specially commissioned half life-size statue mounted on a plinth right outside the trainer's front door.

ALTHREY DON

Grey, 1961, by Fighting Don - Slainte

Owner: John Done
Trainer: Pat Rohan
Jockey: Russ Maddock
Breeder: J.V. Leavy

Former trainer, Pat Rohan, has particularly fond memories of Althrey Don as, unlike some of those other top sprinters with whom he had been associated at Grove Cottage Stables, Malton, including the grey Right Boy, he had actually selected him as a yearling at the sales himself.

Legendary Irish bloodstock agent, Bertie Kerr (his lower lip was permanently attached to a drooping cigarette), who had been responsible for purchasing Right Boy as a yearling, had bid 450 guineas for Althrey Don when he came up for sale as a yearling at Goffs' Ballsbridge Sales in 1962, whereupon the grey was led out of the ring unsold.

In the autumn gloom of that November evening, Pat Rohan then negotiated to buy the grey Fighting Don colt privately at the reserve price of 500 guineas. Six days later he saddled White Smoke, the first horse owned by John Done, to win a selling hurdle at Haydock Park and, after losing the gelding at the subsequent auction, Pat persuaded his owner from Flintshire to have Althrey Don as a replacement.

Twelve months later it seemed a very sound investment as Althrey Don concluded his two-year-old career unbeaten in three starts (all over 5 furlongs), at Ayr, York and Liverpool, although it was the manner of those victories and the fast times recorded, rather than the races themselves, that earned him joint fourth place on the Two-Year-Old Free Handicap.

At three, four and five years, the grey only ran four times per season, the only reason, according to his trainer, being the lack of suitable races in those days. In all three of those years he competed in the Nunthorpe Stakes, winning the all-aged sprint championship as a three-year-old when he made all the running to score by two lengths from Matatina, a bay daughter of Grey Sovereign. In 1965 he finished fourth and in 1966 he was unplaced to the grey Caterina, the previous year's runner-up.

At the end of that season, Althrey Don was bought through the British Bloodstock Agency as a potential stallion for Australia. By the moderate American-bred and Irish-based stallion, Fighting Don, his dam, Slainte, was half-sister to a horse who could hardly have been more different, the black Zarathustra, hero of the 1957 Ascot Gold Cup.

ALYDARESS

Grey, 1986, by Alydar - Balidaress

Owner: Sheikh Mohammed
Trainer: Henry Cecil
Jockeys: Steve Cauthen, Mick Kinane
Breeders: Kinderhill Corporation, Darley Stud Management

Sheikh Mohammed and his Godolphin operation have raced comparatively few greys. Aljabr and Daylami were two distinguished colts to carry the Godolphin blue in the 1990s, but they had been preceded by two star American-bred fillies trained for the Sheikh by Henry Cecil in the previous decade, Indian Skimmer and Alydaress. The former was a four-year-old in training at Warren Place when the latter was an unraced two-year-old.

Whereas Indian Skimmer was in training for four seasons, Alydaress only ever ran as a three-year-old. One of five winners of the prestigious Ribblesdale Stakes for Henry Cecil, she is the only one of the quintet to win the Irish Oaks, sponsored that year by her owner's Kildangan Stud at Monasterevin, Co. Kildare. At the Curragh she defeated the odds-on favourite, Aliysa, who had finished first in the Oaks only to be deprived of victory at Epsom when a routine dope test revealed the presence of camphor.

A lighter grey in appearance than Indian Skimmer, Alydaress had cost Sheikh Mohammed $650,000 at the Keeneland July Selected Yearling Sale when he bought out her other joint breeder, the Kinderhill Corporation. At Keeneland she was consigned from John and Alice Chandlers' Mill Ridge Farm, near Lexington, a well known Kentucky stud with a close affiliation with breeders on this side of the Atlantic.

Alydaress illustrates how the fortunes of a particular female family can be transformed within a few decades. Her dam, Balidaress, who was bred by Charles Haughey, the discredited Prime Minister of Ireland, had been sold for 2,400 guineas as a yearling by Goffs. The winner of three small races in Ireland, she ended her career when defeated in a maiden hurdle at Limerick Junction, hardly the credentials for a top class broodmare!

And what an influential mare she proved. Prior to being sold privately to America, she produced two consecutive winners of the Cheveley Park Stakes in Desirable and Park Appeal. Desirable finished third in the One Thousand Guineas for Catherine Corbett as did another grey, Negligent; she also owned Nicer, who won the Irish One Thousand Guineas.

Alydaress' record as a broodmare is much less distinguished than some of her half-sisters, notably Desirable, the dam of Shadayid (1000 Guineas), another classic winner featured in *Grey Magic*; Park Appeal, the dam of Cape Cross (Lockinge Stakes) and the grandam of Diktat (Haydock Park Sprint Cup); and Balistroika, dam of Russian Rhythm (1000 Guineas).

Cape Cross and Diktat became stallions at Sheikh Mohammed's Kildangan Stud and Dalham Hall Stud respectively. With his first crop of runners, the former sired the brilliant 2004 Oaks, Irish Oaks and Breeders' Cup Filly & Mare Turf heroine, Ouija Board.

ANZIO

Grey, 1957, by Vic Day - Lido Lady

Owner: Sir Thomas Ainsworth, Bart
Trainer: Fulke Walwyn
Jockey: Willie Robinson
Breeder: Harwood Stud Ltd.

When Anzio won the Champion Hurdle as a five-year-old in 1962 he became the youngest horse to win the hurdles' crown since Sir Ken gained the first of three victories at that age in 1952; he is also the first of three greys to win since the war, and the first of two winners saddled by Fulke Walwyn and ridden by Willie Robinson – the other is Kirriemuir.

In later years Anzio alternated between negotiating fences and hurdles albeit he was never as good over the bigger obstacles. He was one half of a big double for greys at Liverpool in March 1961 when Nicolaus Silver won the 'National and he won the Lancashire Hurdle. Newbury was one of his favourite courses, and on his local track he won the Greenham, Berkshire and Wyld Court Hurdles, prior to his Champion victory.

A gelding, who was ideally suited by firm ground, he landed ten hurdle races and three 'chases altogether, but first he had won three flat races in Ireland for his owner, Sir Thomas Ainsworth, when trained by his son, David, on the Curragh – they had acquired the colt as a yearling at Goffs' September Sales at Ballsbridge for 500 guineas.

He was consigned from Milford Stud, Co. Carlow, where his sire, Vic Day, retired to stud as the joint property of Herbert

Blagrave, Anzio's breeder, and stud owner, John Alexander. Later, Vic Day came to stand at Blagrave's Harwood Stud, Woolton Hill, near Newbury, now Sheikh Maktoum Al Maktoum's magnificent Gainsborough Stud.

Herbert Blagrave owned, trained and bred his own horses and presided over a private training establishment beside the A4, west of Marlborough, at Beckhampton Grange, where greyhounds subsequently superceded Thoroughbreds – opposite is the better known Beckhampton House stables where Roger Charlton succeeded his mentor, Jeremy Tree.

A scion of the family which owned Tilehurst Place, Reading, and nearby Calcot Park, Herbert Blagrave was at one time president of Southampton Football Club. With a predilection for French-breds, two outstanding horses to stand at Harwood were Match III and his three-parts brother, Reliance II, both trained in France. Incidentally, Lido Lady, the dam of Anzio, is the ancestress of one of the best mile fillies of 2004 in the French-trained Grey Lilas.

Anzio's sire, Vic Day, who became a noted sire of jumpers, was another horse bred in France. Herbert Blagrave had bought him as a three-year-old on the Wednesday of Royal Ascot in 1948. There was an ultra quick dividend as the following day the colt carried his colours to victory in the King Edward VII Stakes, invariably referred to in the old days as the Ascot Derby.

Anzio last appeared in public as an eight-year-old at Sandown Park in November when as an odds-on favourite he finished last of four. Cath Walwyn explains, "He ruptured his gullet in the race and although he was kept alive by the vets for a few days, it was hopeless and he had to be put down. He always had breathing problems and that is why he favoured fast ground and had to be ridden patiently in all his races so as not to come under pressure until the final furlong or two."

In addition to partnering two Champion Hurdle winners, Willie Robinson was a very polished Irish horseman who also won the Gold Cup on Mill House and the 'National on Team Spirit, both Fulke Walwyn stars, as well as finishing runner-up in the Derby on Paddy's Point; his maternal grandfather, Cub Kennedy, was the breeder of that most famous of all greys, The Tetrarch.

BARON BLAKENEY

Grey, 1977, by Blakeney - Teleflora

Owner: Bob Wheatley
Trainer: Martin Pipe
Jockey: Paul Leach
Breeder: Glebe House Stud

Although Baron Blakeney was a good racehorse in his own right he was an even better one by association as he was the first significant winner saddled by Martin Pipe, whose revolutionary methods have completely transformed the traditional approach to training jumpers.

Baron Blakeney defeated another entire, the favourite, Broadsword, when winning the 1981 Triumph Hurdle at Cheltenham to land a substantial stable gamble off-course at odds of 66-1 – he was completing a hat trick having previously scored over hurdles at Wincanton and Worcester.

An unusually versatile performer, he subsequently justified favouritism in the Great Metropolitan Handicap, then run over the switchback 2 miles 2 furlongs at the Epsom Spring Meeting. As a seven-year-old he scored a memorable victory over fences as a novice when beating subsequent Grand National hero, West Tip, and Gold Cup winner, Forgive 'N Forget, over the Mildmay Course at Liverpool on the opening day of the 1984 'National meeting.

In his time Bill Marshall had excelled with grey cast-offs from big Newmarket stables, notably with Raffingora and My Swanee. The tables were reversed at the 1980 Autumn Sales when Baron

Blakeney, a three-year-old winner at Leicester, made the short trip from Marshall's stable in the Hamilton Road to Park Paddocks where he was retained by Bob Wheatley for 7,800 guineas and promptly joined Martin Pipe, son of a West Country bookmaker.

It was in the same sales ring that the son of Blakeney had been sold as a yearling for 25,000 guineas from Glebe House Stud, Cheveley, then owned by Ingle Thoday, a Cambridgeshire seed grower. Later, the stud would earn a certain notoriety when owner, Alex Scott, the Newmarket trainer, was fatally shot there by his stud groom.

Baron Blakeney became a successful sire of jumpers, particularly point-to-pointers. He stood first at Hart Hill Stud, in Dorset, and then at Sturt Farm Stud, near Burford, in north Oxfordshire. With disruptions caused by the widening of the A40, Roger Stokes then moved his stallions from the Cotswolds to Ireland to Sapperton House Stud, Co. Wexford.

When Baron Blakeney died aged twenty-five in 2002, Martin Pipe said, "We owe a lot to Baron Blakeney as he really set the ball rolling here at Pond House. He was a super, genuine horse and one I will never forget." He was also a great grandson of Abelia, the first horse to feature in *Grey Magic*.

BIRDBROOK

Grey, 1961, by Mossborough - Game Bird

Owner: Alec Pope
Trainer: Michael Pope
Jockey: Ron Hutchinson
Breeder: Moyns Park Stud

Thought to be suffering from a back problem, a wrong diagnosis as it transpired, Birdbrook went to the Newmarket Autumn Sales as a three-year where he was bought cheaply for 1,800 guineas by Michael Pope on behalf of his father, Alec.

That season Birdbrook had scored twice for his breeder, Ivor Bryce, the American owner of picturesque Moyns Park Stud with its thatched roofs, situated near the village of Birdbrook on the Essex-Suffolk border. His trainer at the time was Sam Armstrong, Lester Piggott's father-in-law, from St. Gatien, Newmarket, the yard now occupied by Peter Chapple-Hyam.

Michael Pope, later to become the first president of the National Trainers' Federation, was then based at Wood Farm Stables, Streatley, and Birdbrook became the star of his small but highly successful string. Initially the grey had been bought to go jumping and he did win over hurdles, although it soon became evident that his true forte lay on the flat.

Over the next four seasons the grey proved a confirmed front runner. Hard as nails, he proceeded to win fourteen times on the flat from forty-two starts. Keeping his form well for a seven-year-old entire, he gained his final victory in the Rous Memorial Stakes at Ascot in July on the afternoon of the King George VI and Queen Elizabeth Stakes.

Despite substantial offers from Australia for Birdbrook as a prospective stallion, it was decided to keep him in England and he retired to stand at Dobson's Stud, Fawley, near Henley-on-Thames, just down the road from Streatley. It was an admirable arrangement as Michael Pope managed the stud for his principal patron, Sir Edwin (later Lord) McAlpine, one of whose relations, Bobby McAlpine, raced another distinguished grey in Precipice Wood.

Although Birdbrook was only a handicapper, he sired one particular star in Girl Friend, a top sprinter in France and runner-up in the 1975 One Thousand Guineas to the grey, Nocturnal Spree. Of his grey offspring, Brook, proved a champion miler in Italy and was awarded the 1974 Queen Anne Stakes, the opening event at Royal Ascot, in sensational circumstances. The first three home were disqualified and the name of the first past the post? – Confusion!

A syndicated stallion, Birdbrook died in August, 1979, aged eighteen.

BRUNI

Grey, 1972, by Sea Hawk II - Bombazine

Owner: Charles St. George
Trainer: Ryan Price
Jockeys: Tony Murray, Lester Piggott
Breeder: Barrettstown Estates

Perusing Tattersalls' 1973 October Yearling Sales' catalogue, Charles St. George had marked down Lot 843 as a likely candidate. Unable to attend the sales when confined to bed with 'flu, he instructed his bloodstock partner, Peter Richards, to buy the Sea Hawk colt from Barrettstown Castle Stud in Ireland if he liked him as an individual: only the previous year they had won the Oaks with Ginevra.

The grey was actually knocked down for 7,800 guineas to Irish agent, Jack Doyle, but the purchase did little to hasten St. George's recovery. On seeing the rather light framed yearling in the flesh, he exclaimed, "You bought that! I'll go out and buy you a pair of spectacles." However, Peter Richards had the last laugh as the grey proved an admirable racehorse, winning the St. Leger unchallenged by ten lengths.

Ryan Price was convinced that Bruni was a top-class Cup horse in the making (he did win the Yorkshire Cup), but mindful of the prejudice that commercial breeders have against stayers, his owners determined to exploit him over one-and-a-half miles instead. He did put up some notable performances over that distance, notably when runner-up in the 'King George' to Pawneese, but he never repeated the degree of superiority he had displayed at Doncaster. Stable jockey at Findon, Tony Murray, rode both Ginevra and Bruni to their classic victories.

Repatriated from the USA where he ran without distinction, Bruni stood briefly in Ireland (Ashleigh Stud) and England (Hamilton Stud), before being exported in January 1982 to Kuwait.

Meanwhile his Canadian breeder, Galen Weston of Barrettstown Castle Stud, Co. Kildare (owned previously by American cosmetics queen, Elizabeth Arden Graham), transferred his breeding operation to Bolebec House Stud, near Whitchurch, in the Vale of Aylesbury – this had belonged to Leslie Marler, owner of that good 'chaser, Knucklecracker. Here Galen Weston, developed his Barrettstown Stud (owned nowadays by Pat Eddery), as well as running his Maple Leafs polo team at Windsor.

Galen and his wife, Hillary, were once the subject of a failed, but much publicised, kidnap attempt by the IRA. Along with his late brother, Garry, Galen developed the British and Canadian arms of their vast Wittington food conglomerate which includes Fortnum & Mason and Selfridges in England, and Brown Thomas Department Stores in Ireland. The Weston food dynasty also incorporates Associated British Foods.

Charles St. George, a great personal friend of Lester Piggott, died unexpectedly in May 1992, whereupon his distinctive black colours with a white chevron and cap were taken over by his brother, Edward – he raced a multitude of top horses under the Lucayan Stud label. Both Edward St. George (whose first wife was a sister of bookmaker, William Hill) and Peter Richards died within weeks of one another in 2004. Since then the Lucayan colours have represented Edward's son, Henry, and the latter's uncle, Lord Euston.

Galen Weston and Charles St. George, the principal of Lloyds' underwriting agency, Oakley Vaughan, which specialised in bloodstock insurance, shared an extraordinary link as for short periods both owned Fort Belvedere, near Windsor, where Edward VIII signed the abdication papers.

CALIGULA

Grey, 1917, by The Tetrarch - Snoot

Owners: 6th Earl of Wilton, Mathradas Goculdas
Trainer: Harvey Leader
Jockey: Arthur Smith
Breeder: James Maher

The first of The Tetrarch's three sons to win the St. Leger, Caligula was bred by Jim Maher. One of the most prominent figures of his era in Irish racing and breeding circles, he owned two separate studs outside Dublin in Williamstown, which became part of the late Tim Rogers' Airlie complex, and Confey at Leixlip.

One of few people to breed a Grand National winner, Covertcoat (1913) and a Derby winner, Manna (1925), he also bred Ballymacad, winner of a substitute 'National run at Gatwick during World War 1. Manna also won the Two Thousand Guineas and there were two more classic winners with St. Louis (2000 Guineas), and Sandwich (St. Leger). He is also the breeder of another celebrated grey, Royal Minstrel.

Named after the Roman emperor who allegedly made his horse, Incitatus, a senator, Caligula was owned in turn by two gentlemen whose finances eventually failed to sustain their racing interests.

The first was the Duke of Westminster's kinsman, the 6th Lord Wilton, whose involvement on the Turf was short lived, due to his profligacy and some disobliging creditors. In 1918, within three years of inheriting the title aged nineteen, this Cheshire landowner started buying racehorses on a lavish scale and amongst the yearlings he acquired that year at Tattersalls' July Sales was Caligula for 3,100 guineas.

Unraced as a two-year-old, the grey ran twice at Royal Ascot the following season, winning the Ascot Derby (now King Edward VII Stakes), and finishing third in the St James's Palace Stakes. He was then trained for the St. Leger, but by then his owner was in financial difficulties and a court order prevented him from running his horses, which were duly placed on the open market.

However, the week before the Doncaster classic, a cable to India from Clarence Hailey, a pioneer in racehorse photography, secured a buyer for the colt at 8,000 guineas, with a contingency that the vendor should receive half the stakes in the event of victory – ironically Lord Wilton's great-grandfather had won the 1872 St. Leger with Wenlock.

Success on Town Moor provided classic compensation for his jockey, Arthur Smith, as earlier in the year he had missed winning the Derby on Spion Kop having decided instead to ride the grey Sarchedon, who finished fourth. The previous year Arthur Smith achieved the astonishing feat of riding five winners as an apprentice at Royal Ascot for Frank Barling, whose son, Geoffrey, trained the grey Ascot Gold Cup hero, Erimo Hawk.

Caligula's lucky new owner was Mathradas Goculdas. The biggest cotton mill owner in Bombay, who raced on an enormous scale, he was a Hindu and, although his religion forbade him from leaving the sub continent, it did not curtail his activities as an inveterate gambler. He raced the grey once as a four-year-old in India before he was repatriated to stand the 1922 season at Litchfield Grange Stud, Overton, in Hampshire.

Goculdas ran short of funds too. His extensive bloodstock interests in both England and India were then taken over by Sir Victor Sassoon, who was destined to become one of the pre-eminent owner-breeders in Great Britain. The animals included Star-Belle and to a mating with Caligula she bred the gelded Star of Italy, one of the best horses ever to race in India.

Although his dam, Snoot, just a pony in stature and of no merit on the racecourse, earned international acclaim as a foundation mare, Caligula made little overall impact at stud. Not a fertile horse, he was sold in 1924 to stand in Germany where he died in May 1934.

CALL EQUINAME

Grey, 1990, by Belfort - Cherry Season

Owners: Mick Coburn, Paul Barber, Colin Lewis
Trainer: Paul Nicholls
Jockey: Mick Fitzgerald
Breeder: Kathleen Steele

There was little reason to suppose that the grey foal being led round the sales ring at Doncaster in November 1990 by his breeder, septuagenarian, Kathleen Steele, would become a champion 'chaser.

Had Call Equiname been blessed with a sounder pair of forelegs, the son of Belfort, a sprint handicapper who embarked upon his stud career somewhat incongruously on the Isle of Man, might well have been an eventer – Mrs Steele was the breeder of Merely-A-Monarch, winner of both Badminton and Burghley horse trials in the early 1960s.

Kathleen Steele bred Call Equiname, as well as his dam and grandam, both selling platers, at her home, Colton Grange, a family owned dairy farm between York and Tadcaster. He was the last foal of Cherry Season, who had very nearly died from colic after foaling an own-brother to Call Equiname the previous year.

Sold for 1,700 guineas as a foal, the grey reappeared at Doncaster the following September, but he showed his intermediate owner a loss, realising only 1,500 guineas at the St. Leger Sales. On this occasion he was selected on behalf of Don Eddy, from Ingoe, near Newcastle, by Tommy Robson, a veterinary surgeon and bloodstock agent, who had trained the 1964 Champion hurdler, Magic Court.

"I had bought a yearling and wanted another to keep it company," Don recollected. "So I asked Tommy to pick one out at random as they were going round the ring." After winning two bumper races in Scotland, the gelding, whose sire and dam were both grey, was then resold for a substantial 64,000 guineas at the 1994 Doncaster Spring Sales to join Paul Nicholls in Somerset.

When Call Equiname won the 1999 Queen Mother Champion 'Chase at Cheltenham, coming from behind to beat trail-blazing Edredon Bleu, he was extending his unbeaten record over fences to five. On his previous outing he had won the Victor Chandler 'Chase, which was held at Kempton Park, having been rescheduled from Ascot, not once but twice, on account of the weather.

This represented a major training feat following a 435 days' absence from the racecourse. "We've been tough on him at home this season," commented Paul Nicholls, "and he's taken everything we've thrown at him." In fact a minor injury schooling had initially ruled him out of the Victor Chandler and he was only able to run due to the race being reopened.

A horse who had always suffered from sore shins, Call Equiname had won three of his only four starts over the previous two seasons, since when he had been fired as well as having fibre implants. Although he remained in training for two more seasons, he developed an irregular heartbeat and did not score again – his finale came at Exeter when finishing third in the Haldon Gold Cup despite striking into himself on his off-fore.

It was certainly a great training feat to win a championship event at the Cheltenham festival from only nine lifetime appearances over fences, albeit he always ran well when a fresh horse.

CAMAREE

Grey, 1947, by Maurepas - Couleur

Owner: Jean Ternynck
Trainer: Alexandre Lieux
Jockey: Rae Johnstone
Breeder: Jean Ternynck

In 1950 the French-based Australian-born jockey, Rae Johnstone, known as 'Le Crocodile' for his stealthy technique of pouncing on his opponents unawares, rode the winners of four of the five English classic races.

First he won the One Thousand Guineas in record time on Jean Ternynck's grey Camarée, before partnering Galcador, Asmena and Scratch II to win the Derby, Oaks, and St. Leger respectively in Marcel Boussac's all conquering orange colours with a grey cap. Both owner-breeders were French textile magnates.

Camarée, who had won the Prix Vanteaux at Longchamp prior to Newmarket, as well as two races as a two-year-old, returned to England to compete in the Oaks – she started favourite at Epsom and Gordon Richards had her in front two furlongs from home, only to finish unplaced behind Asmena, whom Rae Johnstone was obliged to ride as Marcel Boussac's retained jockey.

It was from his trainer, Alexandre Lieux, a former champion amateur rider on the flat in France who ran a mixed stable at Maisons-Laffitte, that Jean Ternynck, from Roubaix, near Lille, had procured Camarée's dam, Couleur, the winner of a small hurdle race at Nice where she was also placed over hurdles and fences.

Anything but fashionably bred, Couleur was out of Colour Bar, who had been sold to France in 1936 after winning in England under Pony Turf Club Rules. Fortunately the former survived the German occupation of Normandy to produce not only Camarée but also her own-sister, Marmelade.

Although Marmelade ran only once, she was to prove invaluable in the paddocks as the grandam of Jean Ternynck's homebred champion Sea-Bird II, rated by many as the outstanding racehorse of the 20th century. It is a remarkable fact that none of Sea-Bird's first five dams ever won a race under officially recognised Jockey Club rules of racing in any country.

Unlike Marcel Boussac, who controlled one of the most formidable racing and breeding empires ever assembled in Europe, Jean Ternynck only ever had a handful of broodmares at any one time, but he bred another star in Sanctus, who completed the Prix du Jockey-Club – Grand Prix de Paris double.

CANTON SILK

Grey, 1970, by Runnymede - Clouded Lamp

Owner: W Tsui
Trainer: Peter Supple
Jockey: Greville Starkey
Breeder: John Edmunds

Had Gerald Leigh, owner of estate agents, Hamptons, known as much about bloodstock as he did about property thirty years ago, he would never have bought a grey filly, Canton Silk, as a prospective foundation mare. The experts would have dismissed her out of hand and how wrong they would have been.

Bred by John Edmunds (previously manager to the Macdonald-Buchanans), at his Kingsway Farm, close to Leighton Buzzard and to Lord Rosebery's Mentmore Stud, where his father, 'Tiny' Edmunds, had been manager, the grey daughter of Runnymede realised 2,000 guineas as a foal and 5,700 guineas as a yearling. The very last of 383 lots at the Doncaster St Leger Sales, she was consigned by the late Lord Grimthorpe whose son, Teddy, is now racing manager to Khalid Abdullah.

The filly was purchased by bloodstock agent, John Bartholomew, from Southfleet in Kent, and sent to be trained locally at Dartford by former jump jockey, Peter Supple. Successful three times at two years and once as a three-year-old, all over 5 furlongs, she scored on the Rowley Course at Newmarket as a juvenile at both the Craven and Cesarewitch meetings and was invariably equipped with blinkers.

Gerald Leigh bought Canton Silk privately on his own initiative. "She was owned by a Hong Kong businessman who enjoyed a bet," he recalled many years later. "What I so liked about her was her tremendous determination; she would thrust out her head to the line. She had no pedigree; I paid £22,500 for her in the belief that I could breed the pedigree into her."

Not long after selling Cayton Park Stud at Wargrave-on-Thames and a nucleus of mares to Khalid Abdullah whereupon it became part of Juddmonte Farms, Gerald Leigh purchased Eydon Hall Farm just north of Banbury which he developed into a magnificent private stud and Canton Silk was one of three original broodmares that made the journey up to Northamptonshire in the days before the M40 existed.

"The interesting thing about Canton Silk is that all her foals were natural leaders in the paddock," Gerald Leigh reflected. "Whether they were colts or fillies each of them took charge of the group they grew up with." And the most significant of them proved to be Brocade.

This daughter of Habitat won the Group 1 Prix de la Foret, and mated with Sadler's Wells bred two Irish classic winners in Barathea (1993 2000 Guineas), and Gossamer (2002 1000 Guineas). The former also won the Breeders' Cup Mile, Churchill Downs, before becoming a leading sire at Rathbarry Stud, Co. Cork.

Following Gerald Leigh's death in 2002, the bulk of his bloodstock was sold privately for a reputed £35m to Sheikh Mohammed, thus depriving Tattersalls' December Sales of a major dispersal. Then in September 2004, Leigh's two children, Robin and Sarah, having sold the Eydon Hall Estate, arranged with the new owner, computer games entrepreneur, Tim Stamper, to board their seven strong broodmare band there; four of them are descendants of Canton Silk.

CASSANDRA GO

Grey, 1996, by Indian Ridge - Rahaam

Owner: Trevor C. Stewart
Trainer: Geoffrey Wragg
Jockey: Michael Roberts
Breeder: John McKay

In 2001, twenty-two of the best sprinters in Europe lined up for the King's Stand Stakes, the 5 furlong championship at Royal Ascot, and two grey fillies dominated the finish, Cassandra Go prevailing over Misty Eyed.

It is often said that there are few opportunities for older females in training, but Cassandra Go just went on improving with age and she was five when winning the King's Stand. Officially that is when fillies automatically become mares, whether they have been covered by a stallion or not.

In the case of Cassandra Go, she was very much a mare as by that time she had a Green Desert filly in utero and, as is so often the case, the effect of being in foal seemed to benefit her both mentally and physically – the rules in Great Britain allow a mare to continue racing for 120 days after conception.

Having gained a first Group victory in the King George Stakes at the previous year's Goodwood festival as well as the Temple Stakes as a prelude to Royal Ascot, Trevor Stewart's filly finally bade farewell to the racecourse in the July Cup, finishing an honourable second to the champion, but ill-fated, sprinter, Mozart.

Cassandra Go has a romantic background. An Irishman, Trevor Stewart had bought her as a foal from her breeder, John

McKay, for 82,000 guineas from his Cleaboy Stud, Co. Westmeath (once owned by the great Yorkshire breeder, Lionel Holliday); that summer her two-year-old half-brother, Verglas, had won the Coventry Stakes at Royal Ascot. His intention was to pinhook her, that is to sell her on as a yearling.

The filly returned to Ireland and she was consigned from James Egan's Corduff Stud, Co. Kildare, to the Houghton Yearling Sales. But, as she was being led round the sales ring, her vendor suddenly had second thoughts and, acting on impulse, bought her back for a not inconsiderable 200,000 guineas.

It was Trevor Stewart's wife who was instrumental in naming the grey filly – her corresponding shopping spree involved a visit to fashionable London jewellers, Cassandra Goad.

Rahaam, the dam of Cassandra Go, certainly did well financially for John and Sue McKay. They bought her in February 1995 for IR20,000 guineas and sold her in December 1998 for 280,000 guineas; in between they also sold two of her foals, own-brothers to Cassandra Go and Verglas, for another 260,000 guineas.

CASTLE MOON

Grey, 1975, by Kalamoun - Fotheringay

Owner: Lavinia, Duchess of Norfolk
Trainer: John Dunlop
Jockey: John Lowe
Breeder: Exors of 16th Duke of Norfolk

The grey Castle Moon was foaled in May 1975 just four months after the death of the 16th Duke of Norfolk – only the preceding year he had achieved a lifetime's ambition by winning the Gold Cup at Royal Ascot (where he had been The Queen's Representative for an unprecedented twenty-seven years), with her half-brother, Ragstone.

Although she only won three insignificant races for Bernard Norfolk's widow, Lavinia, Castle Moon was destined to continue the good fortune at her Angmering Park Stud, near Littlehampton, just a few miles from the family home, Arundel Castle, albeit she had a dipped back and tended to race with an ungainly head carriage.

Anything but a prepossessing individual, Castle Moon's dam, Fotheringay, resulted from the mating of Right Royal V, a commanding looking horse, with the mare, La Fresnes. Winner of the Lowther Stakes, La Fresnes, had been acquired for 17,000 guineas (third top price of the week) at the 1962 Newmarket December Sales.

Reflecting on her purchase, the Duchess recalled, "She belonged to John Derby and had bred little rabbits, but jolly good little rabbits."

John Dunlop says, "Castle Moon herself was small with a marginally dipped back and had bad, curby hocks that were fired as a yearling." Notwithstanding these faults, she was to become the cornerstone of the Duchess' stud operation at Angmering Park, breeding three high-class sons in Moon Madness (St. Leger), Sheriff's Star (Coronation Cup), both colts also won the Grand Prix de Saint-Cloud, and Lucky Moon (Goodwood Cup); and her dam, Fotheringay, produced another good middle distance colt in Castle Keep.

Moon Madness, Lucky Moon and Castle Keep were all trained at Arundel by John Dunlop, but the grey Sheriff's Star, who finished third in the St. Leger, was trained by Lavinia Norfolk's daughter, Lady Anne Herries, at her stables adjoining Angmering Park Stud. Widow of the former England cricket captain, Colin Cowdrey, she also trained Fotheringay's great grandson, Celtic Swing (Prix du Jockey Club), for former BHB chairman, Peter Savill.

Another classic winning descendant of La Fresnes is Michelozzo. He provided Charles St. George with a second St. Leger victory in 1989, but unlike his grey Bruni, Michelozzo was trained in his owner's private Sefton Lodge Stables at Newmarket and scored at Ayr as the final day of the Leger Meeting at Doncaster was cancelled when the ground was declared unsafe.

Lavinia Norfolk's step-father, Lord Rosebery, was the owner-breeder of the grey Oaks heroine, Sleeping Partner. One of the Duchess' favourite anecdotes concerned travelling on the train as a schoolgirl from Buckinghamshire up to Rosebery's other home, Dalmeny House, outside Edinburgh. She was enthralled that all the knives, forks and spoons in the restaurant car bore her initials, LMS – Lavinia Mary Strutt. What a disappointment it must have been to learn about the London, Midland and Scottish Railway!

CATERINA

Grey, 1963, by Princely Gift - Radiopye

Owners: Robin F. Scully, Greville Baylis
Trainers: Sam Armstrong, Staff Ingham
Jockey: Lester Piggott
Breeder: Woodpark Ltd.

Caterina's racing career revolved around the Nunthorpe Stakes, the all-aged sprint championship at the York festival meeting in August; run at weight-for-age, it provides the only opportunity for leading two-year-olds to take on their elders.

A neat, attractive grey, Caterina had cost 1,500 guineas as a yearling from Jim McVey's Woodpark Stud, Co. Meath, now one of Maktoum Al Maktoum's Irish studs. Trained by Staff Ingham at Epsom for Greville Baylis (husband of Katie Boyle, a popular television personality), she had won at Goodwood and Ascot as a two-year-old, when she had also finished runner-up to Polyfoto in the Nunthorpe Stakes.

The rivalry between these two good sprinters continued the next season. Polyfoto confirmed his superiority in beating Caterina for the King George Stakes, Goodwood, but the grey filly gained her revenge in winning the Nunthorpe Stakes. Earlier she had also won the Stewards' Handicap at Epsom, the opening race on the Derby Day card.

Robin Scully had procured Caterina at the conclusion of her two-year-old career for 13,000 guineas at the Newmarket December Sales out of Staff Ingham's Epsom stables. As a rather light framed individual it was by no means certain that she would train on, so her record at three years was a bit of a bonus for her new owner whose real reason for buying her was as a potential broodmare for his Clovelly Farms in Kentucky.

Although based in the USA, Robin Scully is a frequent visitor to Europe. Indeed he has a house, Abbotswood, on the edge of Stow-on-the-Wold in the Cotswolds. A familiar figure at the races and sales, he loves Deauville where his lemon and orange colours were carried to victory in the 1980 Prix Morny by Caterina's grey daughter, Ancient Regime.

Ancient Regime was trained in France and so too was her smart own-brother, Cricket Ball, sire of Lady Cricket. One of the gamest 'chasing mares of recent vintage, she was nominated by Tony McCoy as his all-time favourite from his first two thousand winners. Another celebrity bred by Clovelly Farms is Silver Hawk, one of whose many recent Group winners is Mubtaker – this great grandson of Caterina won the Geoffrey Freer Stakes in three consecutive years from 2002 to 2004.

COLONIST II

Grey, 1946, by Riénzo - Cybèle

Owner: Sir Winston Churchill
Trainer: Walter Nightingall
Jockey: Tommy Gosling
Breeder: E. Nominé

Colonist II was the most popular racehorse in a period of general shortages and deprivation after World War II embodying as he did the bulldog spirit of his owner, Sir Winston Churchill, whose very first horse he was – and the greatest Englishman was in his seventies at the time!

Foaled in France in the last year of the war, Colonist was bred by Monsieur E. Nominé at his Haras des Brévières, Seine-et-Oise, where he also stood his sire, Riénzo, from whom he inherited his grey coat. Unplaced on his only two juvenile outings for his owner-breeder, the colt was acquired after he had finished runner-up on his début the following season in a big field of maidens at Le Tremblay.

It took a forum of three to purchase Colonist on behalf of the war-time Prime Minister for around £1,500 – Carey Foster, MRCVS, his future stud manager at Newchapel Stud, near Lingfield Park; his son-in-law, Sir Christopher Soames; and his Epsom-based trainer to be, Walter Nightingall, known as the Saturday specialist as he was so adept at saddling winners on that particular day of the week.

The French-bred was to carry the pink, chocolate sleeves and cap, with great distinction. The ensuing season he won eight of his eleven starts – the last six were consecutive culminating with the Jockey Club Cup. Then as a five-year-old he was an enormously popular winner of the Winston Churchill Stakes. He was also runner-up in the Ascot Gold Cup and fourth in the inaugural King George VI and Queen Elizabeth Stakes which coincided with the Festival of Britain.

Five years after Colonist won the Winston Churchill Stakes over one-and-three-quarter miles at Hurst Park, the same colours were carried to victory in the Churchill Stakes over one-and-a-half miles at Ascot by that horse's half-brother, Le Prétendant.

A big, well-made horse, with plenty of bone, Colonist was syndicated to stand at Heath Stud, Newmarket, at a fee of £98 – his owner said jokingly that he did not wish to live off the immoral earnings of a horse! He then spent an interim period at Aislabie Stud (now Collin Stud), at Stetchworth on the outskirts of Newmarket and at Southcourt Stud, Leighton Buzzard, before moving to the Royal Studs at Sandringham.

His transfer to Norfolk was fortuitous. The late Queen Mother, who had just had the misfortune to lose her young jump stallion, Le Bel, who stood at Sandringham, was talking one day to Carey Foster and he suggested that she should find a horse like Colonist as a replacement. "Oh, do you think I could get him?" Her Majesty inquired. "I am dining with my daughter tonight and I will ask her if she would have him."

Described as a 'charming character, kind and playful' whilst in training, Colonist proved to be a very different proposition as a stallion according to Sir Michael Oswald, manager of the Royal Studs. "He was very irascible and was a particular handful in the covering yard," he recalls. "He was very impatient and if there was any sort of delay in getting the mare ready, he would throw a tantrum and one had to wait until he had calmed down before starting all over again."

Although Colonist made comparatively little impact as a flat sire, he certainly had a sense of occasion. His son, Collusion, was a first homebred runner and winner for his owner's Newchapel

Stud when scoring as a two-year-old at Ascot in July on 'King George' day, 1956; and on the very last day of racing before Winston died in January 1965, Colonist sired a winner over fences at Warwick.

Colonist, who had displayed a peculiar undulating action reminiscent of a child's rocking-horse, in his racing days, proved a noted sire of jumpers. Stalbridge Colonist was much the best known, while the Queen Mother had another smart grey in Isle of Man's half-brother, Inch Arran, a noted front runner around the metropolitan park courses.

For the last few years of his life their sire was based in Norfolk, south of Sandringham at Tim Finch's Winter Paddocks Stud, Old Buckenham, where he was restricted to half a dozen mares per season; he was put down there in 1973 at the advanced age of twenty-seven.

CRY OF TRUTH

Grey, 1972, by Town Crier - False Evidence

Owner: The Hon. Pearl Lawson Johnston
Trainer: Bruce Hobbs
Jockey: John Gorton
Breeder: The Hon. Pearl Lawson Johnston

Had Pearl Lawson Johnston not been on holiday in Scotland, the land of her forebears, she would never have become the owner-breeder of Cry of Truth, the champion two-year-old filly of her generation.

The background story unfolded in East Lothian. Pearl was staying in North Berwick with an aunt by marriage, who had just transferred a filly, False Evidence, from George Boyd's local Dunbar stable to that of Wilfred Crawford (father of distinguished equine artist, Susan Crawford), who farmed just along the A1 at Haddington.

Formerly a commander in the Royal Navy who had played rugger for Scotland, Wilfred Crawford was a jumping trainer and False Evidence ran four times unplaced over hurdles – she had previously been placed at Musselburgh and Lanark on the flat for George Boyd; somewhat lacking in ability, her next outing in the horsebox had been scheduled for the Kelso horse sales.

Many years later, Pearl revealed that she casually asked the Haddington owner-trainer-breeder (his homebred animals invariably had Lothian as a first name) what the filly might make. "He said £50, whereupon I made an offer of £50 which my aunt duly accepted. If I remember correctly, I wrote out the cheque, but I think she gave it me back."

In 1973 False Evidence's daughter, Melchbourne, named after the Bedfordshire village where Pearl lives, was rated the joint top juvenile filly, but the following season Cry of Truth won five of her six starts, including the Cheveley Park Stakes and Lowther Stakes. Indeed she was unlucky to be beaten after losing ground at the start on her début.

It was widely anticipated that the well named Cry of Truth would provide her trainer, Bruce Hobbs, with a first classic success in the One Thousand Guineas, but after finishing ninth of ten in the Nell Gwyn Stakes at the Craven Meeting she never ran again.

Although her stakes-winning daughter, Integrity, bred Radwell (Solario Stakes), Cry of Truth proved rather a disappointment at stud. Latterly her owner-breeder boarded her mares at The Elms Stud, near her home, where the mare died aged eighteen in May 1990, just a few weeks after foaling a grey colt by the resident grey stallion, Neltino.

The youngest of six children and sister to the 2nd Lord Luke, who lived at Odell Castle in Bedfordshire, Pearl Lawson Johnston has devoted much of her life to good works. Their grandfather, John, made a considerable fortune as the inventor of Bovril, which, from Victorian times, became such an integral ingredient of the British diet in the four corners of the globe.

Pearl's cousin, Tom Blackwell, one of Bruce Hobbs' major backers at historic Palace House Stables in the middle of Newmarket, was also involved with the grocery business as one of the Blackwells of Crosse & Blackwell. Owner of Langham Hall Stud, near Bury St. Edmunds, he raced a star filly in Roan Rocket's daughter, Catherine Wheel.

DAYLAMI

Grey, 1994, by Doyoun - Daltawa

Owners: H.H. Aga Khan IV, Godolphin
Trainers: Alain de Royer Dupré, Saeed bin Suroor
Jockeys: Gérard Mossé, Frankie Dettori
Breeder: H.H. Aga Khan IV

It took Sheikh Mohammed's Godolphin operation ten years, from June 1994 to August 2003, to complete a century of Group/Grade 1 victories in eleven countries, spanning three continents – a major contributor with seven victories was Daylami.

As a five-year-old in 1999 the bonny grey ran in five different countries on three continents to win another of Sheikh Mohammed's initiatives, the inaugural running of the five-race Emirates World Series Racing Championship, capturing three of the four qualifying races in which he competed. The WSRC now comprises thirteen races opening and closing with events at Hong Kong's Sha Tin racecourse.

Daylami's complete winning record at the top level comprised the Poule d'Essai des Poulains (French 2000 Guineas) at three years; the Eclipse Stakes and Belmont Park's Man O'War Stakes at four years; and the Coronation Cup, King George VI and Queen Elizabeth Diamond Stakes, Irish Champion Stakes, and Breeders' Cup Turf at five years.

The manner of some of these victories was devastating – at Leopardstown and Ascot he scored by nine lengths and five lengths respectively, but he probably reserved the most memorable for last. On his finale he became the first European-trained horse to win a Breeders' Cup at Gulfstream Park. This was the third occasion that the meeting had been held in the oppressive humidity of Florida and previously more than thirty horses had tried and failed.

It was in October 1997, following his French Two Thousand Guineas triumph when he was also Group 1 placed on a further three occasions, that Sheikh Mohammed took over the colt from his breeder, the Aga Khan, to strengthen the expanding Godolphin team in Dubai. Thereafter he raced in the distinctive all blue Godolphin colours, an unusual occurrence for any grey.

One might have anticipated Daylami retiring to his owner's Dalham Hall Stud or one of its satellites, but instead he took up residence at his breeder's Gilltown Stud in Ireland, where he was bred and conceived – by then his sire, Doyoun, was ensconced at the Turkish National Stud at Izmit. Daylami stands as the property of a syndicate in which Sheikh Mohammed holds a major interest. In 2004 he was joined at Gilltown by his grey half-brother, Dalakhani, winner of the previous year's French Derby and Prix de l'Arc de Triomphe.

For some inexplicable reason the much lighter grey Daylami never quite caught the public's imagination despite proving a truly international star, but he looks certain to redress the balance in his capacity as a stallion With his very first crop he is responsible for the 2004 Irish Derby hero, Grey Swallow, another *Grey Magic* celebrity. With no Northern Dancer blood he is also something of a rarity amongst top-class stallions.

DESERT ORCHID

Grey, 1979, by Grey Mirage - Flower Child

Owner: Richard Burridge
Trainer: David Elsworth
Jockeys: Simon Sherwood, Richard Dunwoody, Colin Brown
Breeder: James Burridge

Desert Orchid was the greatest steeplechaser of his era and achieved a degree of popularity with the public only matched historically by Arkle, Red Rum and Golden Miller. A veteran of seventy-two starts (including one on the Flat), he won thirty-four times, was second eleven times, third eight times for earnings of over £650,000. To mark his retirement Royal Doulton produced a limited edition statuette and every year he even has his own exclusive calendar.

The grandson of a hunter mare bought by his owner's father, James Burridge, a retired solicitor from Ab Kettleby in Leicestershire, Dessie, as he was known affectionately, was a charismatic front-runner, who, somewhat incongruously, began and ended his career by falling at Kempton Park – on his racecourse début as a four-year-old over hurdles, and on his finale just a week before his thirteenth birthday.

That was in the 1991 King George VI Steeplechase, his sixth consecutive appearance in this mid-season championship, a race he had won in four of the five previous years as well as once finishing runner-up, an unparalleled record on the Sunbury course. His retirement was announced immediately afterwards, exactly twenty-five years to the day after Arkle had run his last race – also in the King George.

It was Arkle and Desert Orchid who dominated a survey by the *Racing Post* in the winter of 2004 to ascertain their readers' favourite racehorse of all time. Between them they accounted for forty-one per cent of the entire vote with victory going to Arkle by less than three per cent.

To some observers Desert Orchid looked much more a hunter than a racehorse, who would certainly have looked the part out with the Quorn or the Belvoir, two celebrated packs of foxhounds local to his Leicestershire home. But looks can be deceptive and it is often forgotten that he was a highly proficient hurdler in his younger days, competing in two Champion Hurdles. A natural front runner, he strode like a colossus over the bigger fences, as brave and fearless as he was flamboyant, earning love and admiration in equal measure.

Initially it was thought that he was a two-miler, but that too proved a misleading assumption. Indeed the individual highlight of his wonderful career came in 1989 when he became the only grey ever to win the Cheltenham Gold Cup. Despite a marked preference for a right-handed track and on ground that had been rendered unsuitably heavy by overnight rain and snow, he made up a length's deficit jumping the last to land a famous victory in the dying strides amid scenes of jubilation which were unbelievable even by Cheltenham standards.

Early in 2005, the *Racing Post* conducted a survey described as the ultimate poll to ascertain the 'One Hundred Greatest Races' of all time. Gradually those candidates were whittled down to a short list of ten and voting then took place to determine the greatest individual race. And the winner was? Desert Orchid's Gold Cup triumph.

David Elsworth wrote, "If the Gold Cup were run at Kempton, Dessie would have won it four times, but as it's run at Cheltenham, I never thought the old boy would do it. What nearly did for Dessie was the final bend, as he never seemed to get the wind in his sails coming round it. But I thought he would win when he got to Yahoo at the final fence – he always fought up the hill and he was in one of his most cussed moods that day."

That season Desert Orchid demonstrated a remarkable degree of versatility as prior to Cheltenham, he won the Tingle Creek 'Chase and Victor Chandler 'Chase, both over two miles, as well as his second 'King George' and the Gainsborough 'Chase, both over three miles. Following that Gold Cup victory his legion of followers nearly suffered apoplexy when he had his first fall over fences, in the Martell Cup over the Mildmay Course at Liverpool, but he lived to fight another day.

An extraordinary tough and courageous racehorse, whose career spanned ten seasons, Dessie won twenty-seven of his fifty starts over fences, other memorable victories including the 1988 Whitbread Gold Cup and the 1990 Irish Grand National at Fairyhouse. Only two of those victories were achieved on a left-handed track and he seemed to have a particular affinity with Sandown, a notoriously stiff course, the Whitbread being one of seven victories there.

His racing career must have spawned thousands of column inches in the national press, not to mention various biographies, and by the end of it all his groom, Janice Coyle, was almost as famous as the horse himself. But there was more to come!

Within a year of his retirement, there was a major scare when in November 1992 Dessie was rushed from his home at Ab Kettleby to the Beaufort Cottage Equine Hospital at Exning, outside Newmarket, where he was operated on successfully for a severe colic. Never before had the clinic been deluged with so many enquiries and get well cards from all over the country. It was an altogether happier occasion when he returned to Exning in 1998 as guest of honour at the official public opening of a new surgical unit there.

Most geldings fade away in retirement, but not Desert Orchid, for whom regular public appearances became a way of life, be it the Cheltenham festival in March, the Malton Open Day at Easter, or at Wincanton for a race named after him in October – a race that subsequently lost prestige when its Grade 2 status was transferred to an event at Aintree. He would also pay occasional visits to David Elsworth at Whitsbury where he was often deployed as a lead horse. Latterly he has spent most time with his scriptwriter owner, Richard Burridge, up on the North Yorkshire Moors, near Whitby.

In 2003 the twenty-five-year-old was the star of the Lambourn Open Day, when he lodged with Upper Lambourn trainer, Jean-Rene Auvray. In a letter to the *Racing Post*, his wife, Alison, wrote, "When he arrived at our yard he walked off the box like any old grey horse. When he saw the cameras from the local TV news he suddenly came alive – head came up, neck arched, ears pricked and on came the old razzle-dazzle. I had tears in my eyes. He's a star and he knows it."

A fleeting reference should also be made to Grey Mirage from whom Dessie inherited his grey coat. As the winner of a couple of Two Thousand Guineas trials in the spring of 1972, he looked as though he might prove yet another rare grey bargain procured by Bill Marshall to go along with Raffingora and My Swanee, but he was not destined to achieve comparable success in terms of races won.

Most unusually Grey Mirage had been sold as a back-end two-year-old out of Bernard van Cutsem's Newmarket stable for 32,000 guineas at the Ascot November Sales, having realised 2,000 guineas as a foal and 4,200 guineas as a yearling. At the time van Cutsem had three juveniles rated in the top half dozen of the Free Handicap and two of them, High Top and Sharpen Up, became very influential sires.

As a lasting testimonial, Philip Blacker's statue of Desert Orchid presides at Kempton Park where for many years this great favourite has made a seasonal pilgrimage on Boxing Day to gallop past the winning post, his personal fan club always ensuring the biggest reception of the day. Few of them would be surprised if the grey ghost of Desert Orchid was to manifest itself upon his final departure to the Elysian Fields.

DRAGONARA PALACE

Grey, 1971, by Young Emperor - Ruby's Princess

Owners: Betty Stein
Trainer: Barry Hills
Jockey: Lester Piggott
Breeder: Robin F. Scully

Robin Scully of Clovelly Farms, Lexington, Kentucky, breeder of Pleasantly Perfect, hero of the Breeders' Cup Classic and Dubai World Cup, features in *Grey Magic* as the owner of the grey filly, Caterina, and the breeder of the grey colt, Dragonara Palace, but there is a further connection between them.

At the 1965 Newmarket December Sales, Robin Scully was seeking potential mares for his stud in America and two fillies on his shopping list had excelled that season, the two-year-old, Caterina, who had finished second in the Nunthorpe Stakes, and the Oaks' third, Ruby's Princess – they cost him 13,000 guineas and 11,500 guineas respectively, big sums in those days.

Both were to make a significant contribution in Europe, Caterina as the dam of Ancient Regime (Prix Morny), and Ruby's Princess as the dam of Dragonara Palace. The latter was sold for only $24,000 as a yearling at Saratoga, but he proved a rare bargain, winning the Richmond Stakes and July Stakes as a two-year-old, when he was also runner-up in the Coventry Stakes, beaten a neck.

It was in the Richmond Stakes that his sire, Young Emperor, from whom Dragonara Palace inherited his grey coat, met with his only reversal as a two-year-old. Like father, like son: both

Young Emperor and Dragonara Palace were ridden in England by Lester Piggott and both disappointed as three-year-olds, albeit the latter won the Thirsk Classic Trial Stakes on his seasonal reappearance.

Dragonara Palace preceded another grey stallion, Petong, at David Gibson's Barleythorpe Stud, near Oakham, in Rutland – he and Robert Percival had acquired a half share in Dragonara Palace the previous October. A successful sire of two-year-olds, his outstanding produce was Crime of Passion. Bred by the Gibson family's Highfield Stud, this filly won the Cherry Hinton Stakes in July 1982, and her sire died prematurely in November aged only eleven from a twisted gut.

That season another Dragonara Palace two-year-old, Flockton Grey, was involved in a celebrated ringer case, when the grey three-year-old, Good Hand, masquerading as Flockton Grey, won at Leicester in March by twenty lengths – a fraud that took more than two years for the perpetrators to be brought to justice.

As a star two-year-old, Dragonara Palace, who was named after an hotel owned by bookmakers, Ladbrokes, of which his owner's husband, Cyril Stein, was managing director, had two unlikely relations in the own-brothers, Salmon Spray, winner of the Champion Hurdle, and Larbawn, twice winner of the Whitbread Gold Cup.

ENVIRONMENT FRIEND

Grey, 1988, by Cozzene - Water Woo

Owner: Bill Gredley
Trainer: James Fanshawe
Jockey: George Duffield
Breeder: Stetchworth Park Stud Ltd.

Very occasionally a top horse alternates between stallion duties and active participation on the racecourse. One of the few instances when this dual role might have been considered at least partially successful was with Bill Gredley's homebred grey, Environment Friend.

It was at the Keeneland Breeding Stock Sale in November 1987 that the owner of Stetchworth Park Stud on the outskirts of Newmarket, purchased the mare, Water Woo, for $45,000 carrying to champion grass horse, the grey Cozzene – the foal she was carrying was Environment Friend. "I went there to spend a million dollars on mares," said Bill Gredley, "and Water Woo was one that appealed to me."

Water Woo had been bred by Connie Burrell out of the 1972 One Thousand Guineas heroine, Waterloo. Married to Peter Burrell, supremo of the National Stud at Newmarket, she was the widow of Richard Mellon, a cousin of Paul Mellon, owner-breeder of the great Mill Reef, the outstanding horse to stand at the National Stud since it moved to Newmarket.

As a three-year-old Environment Friend won the Dante Stakes and the Eclipse Stakes. The following season, after recovering from a troublesome lung infection, he finished third in the Champion Stakes.

In all of the next three seasons he returned to training, with a variety of handlers including stud manager, Nigel Wright, and showed top form after covering mares at Stetchworth. At that time his owner, chairman of the property company, Unex, had a broodmare band of seventy plus; at Dullingham Ley, beyond Stetchworth, he created the Middle Park Stud with full training facilities.

The philanthropic Bill Gredley, a great benefactor to the elderly in the local community, is the proud possessor of the historic iron gates at Ascot which led from the course to the winner's enclosure – he procured these for £280,000 at Sotheby's auction of Ascot memorabilia, with the proceeds going to charity, notably Racing Welfare.

At both five and six years of age Environment Friend finished runner-up in the Coronation Cup, and then as a seven-year-old he was third in the Tattersalls' Gold Cup (now Group 1) at the Curragh. It is certainly a reflection of his general temperament and demeanour that he could fulfil the two duties with equal aplomb.

Bill Gredley, who had retained the grey as a yearling for 23,000 guineas at the 1989 Highflyer (better known as the Houghton) Sales, hardly reaped the rewards he deserved so far as the horse's stallion career was concerned. By the time he was eventually sold to Ireland via Helshaw Grange Stud in Shropshire, he was considered a dual purpose (flat and jumping) sire, which is really neither one category nor the other.

The year after winning the Eclipse Stakes, George Duffield, the doyen of the weighing-room, donned Bill Gredley's 'yellow, black stripes on sleeves, white cap', to win the Oaks, Irish Oaks and St. Leger on homebred User Friendly and he also partnered the brilliant grey filly, Alborada, to both of her Champion Stakes victories.

ERIMO HAWK

Grey, 1968, by Sea Hawk II - Nick of Time

Owner: Shinichi Yamamoto
Trainer: Geoffrey Barling
Jockey: Pat Eddery
Breeder: Kilcarn Stud Ltd.

Erimo Hawk was by Sea Hawk II, sire of the grey 1975 St. Leger winner, Bruni, out of a mare by Nicolaus, sire of the grey 1961 Grand National hero, Nicolaus Silver, two more stars of *Grey Magic*.

One of the British Bloodstock Agency's principal Japanese clients in the late 1960s and early 1970s, a market that had been opened up for them by Ted Corbett, was Shinichi Yamamoto, a businessman, who registered the rather garish colours of pale blue, yellow hoops, red sleeves, and red cap with yellow hoop.

The outstanding horse to carry the Yamamoto silks was Erimo Hawk whom the BBA had acquired as a yearling for 10,000 guineas at the Newmarket December Sales from Ned O'Kelly's Kilcarn Stud, Co. Meath. Under the management of his daughter, Pat O'Kelly, Kilcarn has blossomed into Ireland's premier commercial yearling stud of the present day.

Successful on three occasions as a three-year-old, Erimo Hawk, developed into a formidable stayer the following season, winning the Ascot Gold Cup and the Goodwood Cup, the first to complete the double since the great mare, Gladness, in 1958. He was a disappointing favourite in the third leg of the stayers' triple crown, the Doncaster Cup, before finishing unplaced in the Prix de l'Arc de Triomphe.

The son of Sea Hawk won the Gold Cup via the stewards' room as Rock Roi had the ignominy of being disqualified from first place for the second year running; the awkward decision was fully justified as Rock Roi, who got home by a head, had consistently hampered the runner-up in the closing stages.

Tracing back to Mumtaz Mahal's half-sister, Lady Juror, the dam of Fair Trial, Erimo Hawk's dam was a half-sister to the 1966 Two Thousand Guineas winner, Kashmir II, so he obviously derived an abundance of stamina from his sire, Sea Hawk, also a major player in terms of transmitting the grey line of inheritance.

Shinichi Yamamoto boarded a number of mares with the BBA's Christo Philipson at his Lofts Hall Stud, near Saffron Walden, while those with Pat McCalmont at Gazeley Stud, outside Newmarket, included the smart Matatina for whom he had paid 60,000 guineas, the second top-priced mare at the 1971 December Sales. Like Erimo Hawk, her eventual destination was their owner's native country, Japan.

Sea Hawk likewise ended his days in the Far East, having stood for just four seasons with Tim Rogers in Ireland. He made a singular contribution to *Grey Magic*, as in addition to Erimo Hawk and Bruni, he transmitted his grey colour to Sunbittern, Alydaress, Shadayid, One Man and Iris's Gift.

FLYING WILD

Grey, 1956, by Airborne - Wild Delight

Owner: Raymond Guest
Trainer: Dan Moore
Jockey: Tommy Carberry
Breeder: Harold Boyd-Rochfort

There have been many lavish American patrons on the British Turf, but none more successful than Raymond Guest, who owned two Derby winners during the 1960s in Larkspur and Sir Ivor, as well as L'Escargot, winner of the Grand National and two Cheltenham Gold Cups.

As the American Ambassador to Ireland, Raymond Guest had his jumpers trained by Dan Moore and another of them was the popular grey mare, Flying Wild. She was bred by Harold Boyd-Rochfort of Middleton Park Stud, Co. Westmeath, as was her Derby winning sire, Airborne, from whom she inherited her grey coat.

Flying Wild was bought upon the recommendation of Raymond Guest's bloodstock adviser, Tom Cooper of the British Bloodstock Agency (Ireland), and she duly joined Dan Moore – he had just moved from a yard opposite Fairyhouse racecourse, home of the Irish Grand National, to Ballysax Manor, close to the Curragh, the headquarters of Irish racing.

The mare was held in particularly high esteem by Dan Moore and his wife, Joan, as she provided their son-in-law, Tommy Carberry, with his first major victory in England in the 1964 Massey-Ferguson Gold Cup. The race over 2 miles 5 furlongs retained that title until 1981, and then after a number of different sponsors, it became established as the Tripleprint Gold Cup; since 2004 it has been the Bonusprint.com Gold Cup.

That was only the second running of the Massey-Ferguson – Flying Wild had finished runner-up in the inaugural event. The 1964 renewal in December brought about one of the greatest finishes ever witnessed at Prestbury Park with Flying Wild holding on by a short head from Buona Notte with the immortal Arkle, conceding the winner 32lbs, just a length away in third place.

In March, Flying Wild had started joint favourite for the Grand National only to fall at the first fence. Previously she had won the Stone's Ginger Wine 'Chase under top-weight, but her jumping was not always the most reliable – between Sandown and Aintree she had fallen in the Leopardstown 'Chase, cutting herself so badly on the chest that she required nine stitches.

Flying Wild had her grand finale at Cheltenham in March 1966 when Arkle won his third successive Gold Cup. On the opening day the latter's stable-companion, Flyingbolt, had won the Two Mile Champion 'Chase in which Flying Wild finished third; then, in the final race of the three-day meeting, she gained splendid compensation with a 20-length win in the Cathcart Cup which proved her very last appearance over fences.

"She was a good mare, but she was not terribly successful at stud," commented Joan Moore.   Not even a mating with Raymond Guest's own Derby winner, Sir Ivor, at his Ballygoran Stud in Ireland, worked the oracle and in the end her owner took her back to America.

Meanwhile the Carberry family has kept up the good work. Tommy is a leading trainer in Ireland and Paul has emulated his father as a leading jump jockey – they teamed up to win the 1999 Grand National with Bobbyjo.   Paul's sister, Nina, is an outstanding lady amateur rider.

FURTHER FLIGHT

Grey, 1986, by Pharly - Flying Nelly

Owner: Simon Wingfield Digby
Trainer: Barry Hills
Jockey: Michael Hills
Breeder: Simon Wingfield Digby

When fifteen-year-old Further Flight broke his near-hind leg and had to be put down at Michael Hills' home at Wickhambrook, near Newmarket, where he is buried, the vet in charge was Nick Wingfield Digby. He is a cousin of the gelding's owner-breeder, Simon Wingfield Digby, former owner of Sandley Stud, Gillingham, Dorset, once the National Stud and later Prince Fahd Salman's Newgate Stud; today it is an outpost of Scarvagh House Stud in Northern Ireland.

"We'd had him for two years and it has just been so nice for me to pay a horse back for giving me all those great moments," said his regular partner, Michael Hills. "He became a part of the family." His father, Barry, trained him, first at Manton and then in Lambourn where, on retirement, he had become his hack – understandably he is also Barry Hills' all-time favourite racehorse.

When Further Flight and Michael Hills won a record fifth consecutive Jockey Club Cup in 1995, they returned to a tumultuous reception – the grey's popularity with the public in terms of flat horses was on a par with those other great stayers, Brown Jack, Double Trigger and Persian Punch. The durable grey gained the last of his twenty-four victories at Nottingham where he is commemorated by a listed race over 14 furlongs.

With earnings of £ 1/2m, Further Flight was successful in every season from three to twelve years covering some 140 miles in the process, all as a gelding. Apart from his quintet of victories at Newmarket (he became the first horse to win the same European Pattern race five times), he also won two Goodwood Cups, the Doncaster Cup, the St. Simon Stakes, two Lonsdale Stakes, and the Ebor Handicap.

Little did Further Flight's connections realise what lay in store when this grey was led out of the ring unsold as a yearling as one of the early lots at Tattersalls' 1987 Highflyer (better known as the Houghton) Sales. At the time he was rather an angular, unfurnished individual, who was obviously going to take time to come to hand, but that was something that his owner-breeder was prepared to give.

The Rowley Course at Newmarket was the scene of one of Simon Wingfield Digby's greatest triumphs as he won the Cambridgeshire with Further Flight's dam, Flying Nelly. When he died his apple green and black colours duly passed to his daughter, Lady Hardy. Venetia and her husband, Richard, live at Sandley, in Dorset, and she has continued to have a few of Flying Nelly's homebred descendants in training.

This equine family has another string to its bow as Further Flight's grey half-brother, Neltino, did well as a jumping sire at The Elms Stud in Northamptonshire where he sired one of the distinguished 'chasers featured in *Grey Magic*, Teeton Mill – and another member of the Wingfield Digby clan, Michael, owned the grey Welsh National hero, Kendal Cavalier.

Simon Wingfield Digby obviously had the right priorities. As one of the longest standing MP's of his generation, he pronounced on his retirement, "I must say I do prefer the foals to politicians and the stallions to Cabinet Ministers."

GREY ABBEY

Grey, 1994, by Nestor - Tacovaon

Owners: Roper Family, Norman Furness
Trainers: Howard Johnson, Finbar Murtagh
Jockeys: Graham Lee, Brian Harding
Breeder: Francis Small

Most 'chasers aged eleven are past their prime, but not so Grey Abbey. Trained in Co. Durham by Howard Johnson and invariably equipped with a small sheepskin noseband, he performed better during the 2004/05 season than at any other time, and as a bonny front running grey and a spectacular jumper, he is remarkably reminiscent of Desert Orchid himself.

That season he won three of his four starts, the Charlie Hall 'Chase, Wetherby (when three of the six runners were grey), the Pillar Property 'Chase, Cheltenham, invariably a serious Gold Cup trial, and the Betfair Bowl, over the Mildmay Course at the Liverpool Grand National Meeting, to prove one of the most popular and consistent three-mile 'chasers in training.

On his only other start he finished a gallant fifth in the Gold Cup despite an interrupted preparation (he had rapped a front joint in winning at Cheltenham), and on ground that was unsuitably fast. The original intention had been to retire him after the Gold Cup, but his subsequent victory at Aintree (he was a late withdrawal from the 'National itself), brought about an entirely new appraisal and it was planned to keep him in training for the 2005/06 season.

Previously Grey Abbey had registered all his successes in the north, highlighted by the 2004 Scottish Grand National which he won by a distance under top-weight – his sixth victory over fences at Ayr. Having also won the Grand National on Amberleigh House, Graham Lee became the first jockey to complete that particular 'National double in the same season since Brian Fletcher thirty years earlier on Red Rum – both Amberleigh House and Red Rum were trained by Ginger McCain.

Finbar Murtagh, who trains near Carlisle (he rode for Jonjo O'Neill when he was based at Penrith), had procured the grey originally for his owners, local dairy farmers from Abbeytown (which helps explain the name), at a time when Cumbria was devastated by the foot and mouth epidemic. Then an unbroken four-year-old, he cost 12,000 guineas at the Doncaster Spring Sales of 1998. Consigned from Co. Antrim, he was described in the catalogue as a chesnut.

The gelding inherited his grey coat from his sire, Nestor (by Nishapour). A useful staying handicapper, he was purchased cheaply as a six-year-old at Doncaster Sales en route to Ratley Lodge Stud, near Banbury, in Oxfordshire, owned by Peter Thorne – his brother, John, a noted amateur rider, used to stand a number of jumping stallions at his Chesterton Stud in Warwickshire. The stallion was then sold to Francis Small of Cookstown, Co. Tyrone, in Northern Ireland, the breeder of Grey Abbey.

Remarkably none of Grey Abbey's first three dams ever ran, far less won, but nonetheless he shares the same grandam with another very smart grey in The Grey Monk and he was also trained in Cumbria, by Gordon W. Richards.

GREY SOVEREIGN

Grey, 1948, by Nasrullah - Kong

Owners: Frank Measures, Jack Measures
Trainer: George Beeby
Jockeys: Harry Carr, Ted Fordyce
Breeder: William Hill

There is a certain irony about Grey Sovereign, who became not only a successful sire in his own right, despite being a whistler (a particular wind infirmity in horses usually regarded as hereditary), but also an even more successful sire of sires; his breeder, William Hill, procured a number of potential stallions for his Whitsbury Stud, none of whom ever came up to expectations.

William Hill, 'The World's Biggest Bookmaker', was an uncle of Christopher Harper, the present owner of Whitsbury, near Fordingbridge, in Hampshire. Grey Sovereign's trainer, George Beeby, from Compton in Berkshire, son of a well known horse dealer in the 'shires, was at one time private trainer to Lord Bicester for whom he trained such magnificent 'chasers as Silver Fame (chesnut not grey), Roimond and Finnure. He is the father of Harry Beeby, chairman of Doncaster Bloodstock Sales, whose son, Henry, is the current managing director.

It was Phil Bull, the founder of *Timeform*, who bought the grey Wokingham Stakes heroine, Kong, for William Hill for just 710 guineas at the 1943 December Sales and she later produced Nimbus. The first yearling he ever sold, he won the 1949 Two Thousand Guineas and Derby. That year his three-parts brother, Grey Sovereign, came under the hammer as a yearling, but during the inevitable inspection by Nimbus's trainer, George Colling, the colt tried to kick him.

Grey Sovereign's temperament caused concern throughout his lifetime. As a two-year-old he was frequently ridden in the paddock preliminaries and was often accompanied to the start by the trainer's assistant whose unenviable task was to help the horse relax by pulling his tongue. Never inclined to do anything against his will, such stubbornness persisted into old age when he would sometimes defy all attempts to bring him in from the paddock. If rearing up and striking out failed to have the desired effect, he would charge with teeth bared.

The son of Nasrullah, from whom he inherited these wayward tendencies, was purchased for 6,700 guineas at Tattersalls' July Yearling Sales at Newmarket by Frank Measures, a sporting farmer from Lincolnshire. After his first four starts, he raced for his brother, Jack, a Skegness hotel proprietor for whom he won that season's Richmond Stakes and was runner-up in the Coventry Stakes.

In sharp contrast to Nimbus, Grey Sovereign actually finished last in a field of twenty-seven in the Two Thousand Guineas. Ridden by Martin Molony, who was associated with all those marvellous 'chasers belonging to Lord Bicester, he pulled up in a distressed condition. It transpired that he had sustained cracked ribs, probably inflicted when kicked by another runner down at the start; four months elapsed before he appeared again in public.

In due course he was to prove a proficient, if somewhat erratic, sprinter. As a four-year-old he won the Festival Stakes at now defunct Birmingham from Royal Serenade, placings that were reversed in the Nunthorpe Stakes. In the King George Stakes and Diadem Stakes he was reluctant to start, while in the King's Stand Stakes he dug his toes in for a second time that season and refused to take any part in the proceedings.

It was not a record which gave any indication of the enormous influence that he would exert as a stallion. Not only did he sire a string of fast horses, but he also formulated a whole dynasty of stallions around the globe to become one of the key links in the Nearco/Nasrullah male line. Three of his stallion sons to feature in *Grey Magic* are Raffingora, Sovereign Path and Young Emperor - Jack Measures bred another good one at his Croft Grange Stud in Sovereign Lord (Gimcrack Stakes, Richmond Stakes), but he was a bay.

Grey Sovereign retired to stud at Derisley Wood Stud, Newmarket, before moving to Jim Philipps' stud in the village of Gazeley, which, rather confusingly, was then known as Dalham Hall (once owned by Cecil Rhodes) before it became Gazeley Stud. On his arrival there he was accompanied by two handlers, such was his reputation as a difficult customer. But despite his idiosyncrasies, Jack Measures always thought the world of him.

In view of his erratic behaviour on the racecourse, the probability is that Grey Sovereign would have been gelded but for his close relationship to Nimbus. A stallion whose stud fee had escalated from £148 to £1,750 (making him the highest priced stallion in the country), he was sold when seventeen years of age to a company registered in the Bahamas, for £175,000. Subsequently he was transferred to Bergh Apton Stud, near Norwich, owned by bloodstock agent, Keith Freeman.

Although completely deaf in old age, the horse survived four days past his twenty-eighth birthday. He was duly buried at Bergh Apton – his final resting place was the centre of Tattersalls' old open-air sales ring in Park Paddocks through which he had been sold as a yearling and which had found a new home in Norfolk.

Coincidentally, Jack Measures and Jim Philipps, two people so closely involved with Grey Sovereign, ended their lives in tragic circumstances – both were found with fatal gunshot wounds.

GREY SWALLOW

Grey, 2001, by Daylami - Style of Life

Owners: Rochelle Quinn, Murry Rose Bloodstock
Trainer: Dermot Weld
Jockey: Pat Smullen
Breeder: Marguerite Weld

A certain 'grey swallow' certainly made it a summer to remember for the Weld family as the colt of that name won the 2004 Irish Derby at the Curragh beating the odds-on favourite, North Light, winner of the Derby at Epsom three weeks earlier, by a convincing half length.

Trainer Dermot Weld, MRCVS, who was repeating his Irish Derby victory with Zagreb eight years earlier, had been uncharacteristically optimistic about Grey Swallow's chances, despite the fact that he had never raced beyond a mile – previously he had finished fourth in the Two Thousand Guineas at Newmarket and third in the Curragh equivalent.

Undefeated in two juvenile starts, both over 7 furlongs, the grey son of Daylami had been rated the leading two-year-old of his generation in Ireland, but his racecourse career had started ominously. On his intended début at the 2003 Derby fixture at the Curragh, he became wedged over the central partition of the starting stalls and had to be withdrawn in what was a very scary incident.

Dermot Weld, who has earned international acclaim with his runners in both hemispheres, refers to Grey Swallow as "the family horse" and rightly so. Racing originally in the colours of

Rochelle (Shelley) and Tommy Quinn from New York, he was part owned by Dermot Weld's mother, Marguerite, and Terry Ramsden, whose own colours were carried to victory by Katies in the 1984 Irish One Thousand Guineas.

Grey Swallow was bred by Gita Weld at her Pipers Hill Stud, Naas, Co. Kildare, whence he was consigned to the Houghton Yearling Sales at Newmarket, realising 150,000 guineas en route to her son's Rosewell House stables, just a stone's throw from the Curragh racecourse. Gita, the widow of trainer, Charlie Weld, bought Pipers Hill in 1968 when moving from Glenvale Stud, Carrick-on-Suir, Co. Tipperary. The first good horse they bred was Grand Prix de Paris hero, Roll of Honour.

Previously Pipers Hill was owned by Frank Darrell Farmer, who not only trained his own horses but also bred them too. Another to be bred and raised there was the 1970 Grand National hero, Gay Trip. Frank Farmer also sold Owen's Sedge, a smart grey 'chaser of the 1950s, to Hollywood film star, Gregory Peck.

Belonging to the first crop of Daylami from whom he inherits his grey coat, Grey Swallow hails from a long line of American-bred mares going back to Stolen Hour. Her descendants include a host of European celebrities including Spinning World, and the own-brothers, Try My Best and El Gran Senor.

On the conclusion of his three-year-old career, a ninety per cent share in the Daylami colt was sold to Geneva-based Jean Pierre Regali with Gita Weld retaining a ten per cent share. The new partnership, racing as Murry Rose Bloodstock got off to the best possible start in '05 when, back at the Curragh, the scene of his greatest triumph, the colt defeated the previous year's 'Arc hero, Bago, for the Tattersalls' Rogers Gold Cup.

After disappointing in his midsummer target, the 'King George' run at Newbury where he sustained a cut hind leg, Grey Swallow's trainer intimated that all being well his autumn campaingn would focus on the USA with the Man O'War Stakes, Turf Classic and Breeders' Cup Turf, all at Belmont Park, as likely objectives.

HABAT

Grey, 1971, by Habitat - Atrevida

Owner: Dr. Carlo Vittadini
Trainer: Peter Walwyn
Jockey: Pat Eddery
Breeder: Marston Stud

Just before Dr. Carlo Vittadini's colours became really well known with champion Grundy, the Milanese owner had a very good two-year-old called Habat. The grey had been acquired by his racing manager, Norwich-based bloodstock agent, Keith Freeman, for 14,500 guineas at the Houghton Sales from Marston Stud where he was bred.

Buried there in the hamlet of Marston St. Lawrence, near Banbury, in north Oxfordshire, are two Grand National winners, Reynoldstown (1935/1936), and Well To Do (1972). It was from Reynoldstown's owner-trainer, Noel Furlong, that John Sumner bought Marston House, and his late wife, Heather, bequeathed Well To Do to his trainer, Tim Forster, in her will – she died the year before the horse's great Aintree triumph.

Reynoldstown gained the first of his two 'National victories ridden by Noel Furlong's son, Frank. On the second occasion his successful partner was another amateur, Fulke Walwyn, the celebrated jumps trainer to be, who was a cousin of Habat's trainer, Peter Walwyn.

"My wife wanted another interest when our two daughters, Joanna (Wellesley) and Tocky (Mckie), had grown up," recalled John Sumner, "and she decided to breed horses for the flat. I suppose we had as many as eleven mares at one time."

One of those mares was the beautifully bred Atrevida, whom Keith Freeman had bought at the 1968 Newmarket December Sales for 31,000 guineas from her breeder, the Aga Khan. Third in the Irish One Thousand Guineas, she was a daughter of another *Grey Magic* celebrity in Palariva. The latter's dam, Rivaz (Queen Mary Stakes, July Stakes), was an own-sister to Nasrullah.

Habat was rated the top English trained two-year-old of his generation, winning the Norfolk Stakes (Royal Ascot), by six lengths, Mill Reef Stakes, by five lengths, and Middle Park Stakes, by two-and-a-half lengths. On his début at Kempton Park (rescheduled from Sandown), he had been beaten a neck by another distinguished grey juvenile in Dragonara Palace.

Successful on his seasonal reappearance in the Two Thousand Guineas Trial at Ascot, Habat could only manage sixth place in the Newmarket classic, but was subsequently runner-up in the Sussex Stakes. The fates conspired against him that season, and two intended appearances at Ascot were called off at the last moment. He missed the St. James's Palace Stakes due to a skin rash and the Queen Elizabeth II Stakes when the meeting was cancelled – the course was waterlogged due to incessant overnight rain.

Notwithstanding these disappointments, there was considerable optimism when Habat retired to stand at the National Stud for the 1975 covering season, but like so many sons of Habitat he failed to make the grade as a stallion and was exported to Japan in 1981 – he had spent his last four seasons in Newmarket at his owner's Beech House Stud (now owned by Sheikh Hamdan Al Maktoum) where the great Nearco is buried.

HULA DANCER

Grey, 1960, by Native Dancer - Flash On

Owner: Mrs. Peter Widener
Trainer: Etienne Pollet
Jockeys: Roger Poincelet, Jean Déforge
Breeder: Mrs. Peter Widener

From his very exclusive stables at Chantilly, Etienne Pollet trained two winners of the One Thousand Guineas within the space of four years for American lady owner-breeders, Never Too Late II who also won the Oaks in 1960 , and Hula Dancer in 1963. Both were partnered by Roger Poincelet.

A tall grey, a shade on the leg whilst in training and the first of her sex to win over £100,000 in Europe, Mrs. Pete Widener's Hula Dancer won all three of her starts as a juvenile, the Prix Yacowlef at Deauville, Prix de la Salamandre and Grand Criterium, all with consummate ease. Remarkably she was the last of eight consecutive winners of the Salamandre for her trainer. Most unusually for a filly, she headed the Handicap Optional.

Justifying odds of 2-1 on in the One Thousand Guineas by a length from Spree (the short price reflected a facile victory in the Prix Imprudence on her seasonal reappearance), Hula Dancer was aimed at the French rather than the English Oaks. Disappointing when fifth in the Prix de Diane, she then reverted to a mile, gaining impressive wins in the Prix Jacques Le Marois at Deauville and the Prix du Moulin de Longchamp.

It was generally considered that her failure in the French Oaks, the solitary defeat of her career, was due to lack of stamina, so it caused quite a surprise when connections decided on a return visit to Newmarket for the Champion Stakes over 10 furlongs, just a $^1/_2$ furlong less than the Chantilly classic. But her devastating acceleration entering the Dip won the day, as she repulsed the black Irish invader, Linacre.

Hula Dancer was just one of a number of famous horses with whom Mrs. Widener was associated. Her husband, owner of the famous Elmendorf Farm in Kentucky, had actually given her Hula Dancer's grandsire, Polynesian, as a wedding anniversary present, while her runners in France also included Dan Cupid, the sire of Sea-Bird II, and Grey Dawn, the only horse ever to defeat this great champion.

Two years before Mrs. Widener's death in New York in 1970, all her French-based bloodstock had been sold at a dispersal at the Deauville November Sales. Heading the twenty-five lots was Hula Dancer. Having opened the bidding at one million francs, Raymond Guest secured her for 1.02m francs (£86,000), whereupon the audience broke into spontaneous applause. This more than doubled the previous European auction record for a broodmare.

Initially, Hula Dancer went to her new owner's Ballygoran Stud, Maynooth, Co. Kildare (now owned by Sheikh Hamdan Al Maktoum), which he had bought to stand Larkspur, who was replaced in turn by Sir Ivor, the respective Derby winners of 1962 and 1968. At the time her owner reflected, "Since Sir Ivor gave her to me, I shall return the compliment and give her to Sir Ivor. She will be one of his first mates."

There was a sting in the tail, however. It transpired that Hula Dancer was barren to Sir Ivor when shipped to the USA in 1970 and the Val de Loir colt that she was carrying when Raymond Guest bought her proved to be her third and final offspring and none of them ever won a race.

Hula Dancer inherited her grey colouring from her sire, Native Dancer. One of the all-time greats of the American turf, his influence lives on, as he is the grandsire of two exceptional stallions – his son, Raise A Native, sired Mr. Prospector, and his daughter, Natalma, produced Northern Dancer. Native Dancer is also the sire of Secret Step and the grandsire of Saritamer, two more *Grey Magic* stars.

HUMBLE DUTY

Grey, 1967, by Sovereign Path - Flattering

Owner: Jean, Lady Ashcombe
Trainer: Peter Walwyn
Jockeys: Lester Piggott, Duncan Keith
Breeder: Frank Tuthill

At Tattersalls' Houghton Yearling Sales in 1968, Charles Smith-Bingham of the now defunct British Bloodstock Agency, bought a daughter of Sovereign Path consigned by Frank Tuthill's Owenstown Stud, Co. Kildare, in Ireland, on behalf of his mother, Jean, Lady Ashcombe, and the grey duly went into training with Peter Walwyn in Lambourn.

Humble Duty, as she became known, was the most expensive filly of the week at 17,000 guineas as she was a beautiful individual with an attractive pedigree, but there are always detractors, as her trainer recalls. In this particular instance they ranged from the suggestion that she had defective vision to the fact that she was bred to get only three furlongs!

Needless to say such adverse comments were totally without foundation and by the close of her two-year-old career the grey was rated the best of her age and sex, having won both the Lowther Stakes and the fillies' end of season championship, the Cheveley Park Stakes. A bout of sore shins in mid-season may have contributed to her finishing only third in the Queen Mary Stakes.

Unlike so many top juvenile fillies, she then proved just as good the ensuing season. An outstanding miler, she won the One Thousand Guineas by a commanding seven lengths, a record margin for the 20th century and her trainer's first classic victory. Successful in the Coronation Stakes at Royal Ascot, she then demolished the colts in two summer spectaculars at Goodwood, the Sussex Stakes and Wills' Mile, starting favourite on both occasions.

The first filly to win the Sussex Stakes since the celebrated grey Petite Etoile in 1959, Humble Duty was also the first to bring off the Sussex Stakes – Wills Mile (later Celebration Mile), double. On both occasions at Goodwood she was partnered by stable jockey, Duncan Keith – he had been reunited with the filly having forfeited the ride in the Guineas to Lester Piggott due to weight problems.

Humble Duty, whose sire, Sovereign Path, and maternal grandsire, Abernant, are two other celebrities in *Grey Magic*, retired to her owner's Attington Stud, near Thame, in Oxfordshire, where she died from the combined effects of a stomach rupture and blood clot without making her mark in the paddocks, apart that is from the sale of her first foal, a Tudor Melody colt, who topped the Newmarket October Sales of 1973 at 37,000 guineas.

Unfortunately in March of that year Jean Ashcombe and her sister, Elizabeth Thursby, had been killed in an air disaster over Nantes on returning from holiday in Majorca. A keen rider to hounds in Warwickshire where she was brought up, Jean had owned a few jumpers pre-war. These included the 1939 Cheltenham Gold Cup hero, Brendan's Cottage, who was trained by George Beeby, the handler of that most influential of greys, Grey Sovereign.

It was to Grey Sovereign that Humble Duty's breeder, Frank Tuthill, bred La Tendresse, the champion two-year-old in England and Ireland in 1961. Like another fine juvenile by Grey Sovereign, the grey Young Emperor, she was trained by Paddy Prendergast Snr. for the American, Pansy Parker Poe.

INDIAN SKIMMER

Grey, 1984, by Storm Bird - Nobiliare

Owner: Sheikh Mohammed
Trainer: Henry Cecil
Jockeys: Steve Cauthen, Michael Roberts
Breeder: Ashford Stud & Ron Worswick

Indian Skimmer was a brilliant racemare who has proved, to date at least, a failure at stud. It is not an uncommon phenomenon and one that is frequently attributed to being too masculine, a quality enabling a female to hold her own at the highest level on the racecourse, but which somehow compromises her breeding potential.

There are obvious comparisons here with another legendary grey filly in Petite Etoile, who was likewise trained at Warren Place, by Henry Cecil's predecessor and former father-in-law, Noel Murless – and, like Petite Etoile, Indian Skimmer, who cost Sheikh Mohammed 350,000 guineas as a yearling, remained in training until she was a five-year-old and excelled over 10 furlongs.

The American-bred grey retired to stud as the winner of ten of her sixteen races and never finished out of the first four. During the early part of his training career Henry Cecil rarely ran horses abroad, but Indian Skimmer gained three of her five Group 1 victories in France ridden by the popular American stable jockey, Steve Cauthen. Unbeaten in five starts at three years, she won the Prix de Diane, beating another star filly in Miesque by four lengths.

That season she also won the Prix Saint-Alary, then gained further Group 1 victories at four years in the Champion Stakes in both England and Ireland, ridden on both occasions by multiple South African champion, Michael Roberts, and the Prix d'Ispahan at five years.

Despite her commendable consistency on the racecourse, she experienced her share of setbacks in training and after her French Oaks victory she was off the course for almost a year with back and shoulder problems. Latterly she did not relish being asked to race on firm ground which was ill suited to her slightly round action.

Just like Petite, Etoile Indian Skimmer could be idiosyncratic: with the fair sex brilliance and temperament frequently go hand in glove. In that respect she was fortunate to be trained by someone as sympathetic and understanding as Henry Cecil. who was always prepared to cajole and lend encouragement when the occasion arose – prior to her Champion Stakes victory at Newmarket, for example, when he painstakingly led her all the way down to the start.

At the conclusion of her four-year-old career, Henry Cecil went on record as saying, "On the right ground I have never had anything like her and I think she is still improving. I have trained some very good animals, but she is brilliant. It would be unfair to her not to say she is the best I have ever had – and that includes the colts."

Retrospectively Henry Cecil is not to be drawn as to which of his brilliant fillies, Oh So Sharp, Indian Skimmer and Bosra Sham, was superior, so it is obviously a close call. However, Indian Skimmer has a unique claim to fame. Her distinctive grey line goes back at six generations to the Eclipse hero, Royal Minstrel, a relatively obscure sire in Great Britain, who was the first top horse trained by Henry's step-father, Cecil Boyd-Rochfort.

IRIS'S GIFT

Grey, 1997, by Gunner B - Shirley's Gift

Owner: Robert Lester
Trainer: Jonjo O'Neill
Jockey: Barry Geraghty
Breeder: Ann Crank

When Best Mate emulated Arkle in winning three consecutive Cheltenham Gold Cups, one of few rising stars who could be given serious consideration as a potential adversary for the 2005 renewal was a magnificent grey who had yet to jump a fence in public, albeit he was reputed to have schooled brilliantly at home.

Trained just down the road from Cheltenham at Jackdaws Castle by Jonjo O'Neill, who famously rode the mare, Dawn Run, to victory in the Champion Hurdle and the Gold Cup during the mid-1980s, Iris's Gift concluded the 2003/4 season as the winner of eleven races, the first three in bumpers, from a career total of sixteen starts.

The extraordinary aspect of the grey's innings thus far was that whatever he had achieved over hurdles was a bonus. His physique and jumping ability (his technique was indifferent at first but it soon improved) had earmarked him out as a potential 'chaser and there was the added bonus that he had not only proved himself over Cheltenham's unique terrain, but also that he stayed three miles.

As a six-year-old he had finished runner-up to Baracouda in the Stayers' Hurdle prior to winning the Sefton Novices' Hurdle at Aintree. The following season he reversed the tables with the French champion in what is now called the Ladbrokes World Hurdle, before gaining another memorable victory at the Grand National Meeting, this time in the revamped Liverpool Hurdle, a new name for the Long Distance Hurdle transferred from Ascot.

However, Jonjo O'Neill's stable was ravaged by the virus during the 2004/05 season and in the end Iris's Gift's made just one solitary appearance. In February on his début over fences in the Ascot 'Chase (transferred to Lingfield), he was last of the five finishers. Four weeks later both he and Best Mate were absentees from the Gold Cup won by the grey's regular partner, Barry Geraghty, aboard the Irish star, Kicking King.

Robert Lester, the owner of Iris's Gift, named him after his late mother and the former coal merchant from Cheshire bought the gelding locally for £5,000 from Tattenhall breeder, Ann Crank, as a four-year-old out in the field. "He looked big and backward," she recalled, "and we never thought that he would be racing as soon as he did." Ann and her husband, Reg, a former jump jockey, run a breaking and point-to-point yard.

Both Iris's Gift's sire, Gunner B, Britain's top jumping sire of the 1990s, and his maternal grandsire, Scallywag, used to stand in this part of the country. It is from Scallywag, that he inherits not only his grey coat, but also his imposing physique. One of a number of useful greys bred by Dorothy de Rothschild at her Waddesdon Stud, Scallywag stood all of 17.2 hands and could only just be accommodated in the starting stalls.

Unraced Shirley's Gift, the dam of Iris's Gift, was bred by Reg Crank's mother, Pam, and he was one of her only three foals. The grandam, Earlsgift, on whom Reg's brother, Simon, won three point-to-points in the space of a week, was a half-sister to top hurdler, Browne's Gazette.

This is a typical National Hunt rags to riches story. The breeder of Earlsgift actually sold her as a four-year-old at Ballsbridge in 1980 for just 640 IRguineas and Iris's Gift's owner turned down an offer of £1m for the grey – some price for a gelding!

JOJO

Grey, 1950, by Vilmorin - Fairy Jane

Owner: Joe Childs
Trainer: George Digby
Jockey: Vic Mitchell
Breeder: J.R. Neill

In the spring of 1962 The Queen's racing manager, Lord Porchester, lost a mare booked to visit Doutelle at the Royal Studs. Searching for a quick replacement, he prevailed upon George Stephens of Shaw Park, near Plumpton, in Sussex, to sell his grey mare, Jojo, privately.

Jojo was within weeks of foaling to a totally unfashionable sire in Clear River. However, Henry Porchester had some valuable inside information. At the time, his father, the 6th Lord Carnarvon, owned two of Jojo's offspring, Scots Fusilier, who had scored four times as a two-year-old the previous season, and his year junior own-brother, Queen's Hussar, then showing plenty of promise on the gallops.

Queen's Hussar proved an admirable racehorse, winning the Sussex Stakes and Lockinge Stakes. He also became a champion sire based at Highclere, thanks to Brigadier Gerard, one of the great horses of the 20th century, and The Queen's Highclere (1000 Guineas and French Oaks), dam of Sheikh Hamdan Al Maktoum's famous broodmare, Height of Fashion; she in turn produced Nashwan, Unfuwain and Nayef, all of whom retired to stand at his Shadwell Stud in Norfolk.

Highclere Stud is situated in the grounds of Highclere Castle, on the borders of Hampshire and Berkshire, south of Newbury, and the house contains some priceless Tutankhamun artefacts – Henry Porchester's grandfather was the famous Egyptologist and patron of Howard Carter, who discovered the Pharaoh's tomb and, by sheer coincidence, Jojo was trained by George Digby, who had himself trained in Egypt.

George Digby had procured Jojo as a yearling from her breeder at Newmarket in January 1951 for 210 guineas. After winning as a three-year-old at Lingfield Park in the colours of that great between the wars jockey, Joe Childs, she was then bought back at that year's July Sales for 1,500 guineas. She reappeared in the Newmarket sales ring in each of the next two years making 530 guineas and then 200 guineas.

It seems inconceivable that Worksop Manor Stud received less for Jojo in foal than when buying her out of training, but she proved an amazingly successful foundation mare for the 7th Lord Carnarvon, principally through her daughter, Hiding Place – she resulted from the mating with the ill-fated Doutelle, who died tragically at Sandringham when he got entangled in his rack-chain.

Just to illustrate the versatility of the family, Hiding Place became the dam of Little Wolf, who triumphed for his breeder in the 1983 Gold Cup over two-and-a-half miles at Royal Ascot, and the grandam of Sheikh Albadou, winner of the 1991 Breeders' Cup Sprint over 6 furlongs at Churchill Downs. Jojo produced twelve winners from sixteen foals; and seven of Hiding Place's sons became stallions in various parts of the world.

There are still representatives of the Jojo family at Highclere, which is managed by the late Lord Carnarvon's daughter, Lady Carolyn Warren, wife of bloodstock agent, John, and they added to the long list of Group winners descending from Jojo when Captain Hurricane won the 2004 July Stakes.

KALAGLOW

Grey, 1978, by Kalamoun - Rossitor

Owner: Anthony Ward
Trainer: Guy Harwood
Jockey: Greville Starkey
Breeder: Someries Stud

Routine blood-typing and microchipping of foals by the Jockey Club secretariat, Weatherbys, should eliminate the possibility of mistaken identity so far as registration in the *General Stud Book* is concerned, but remarkably Kalaglow, one of the leading horses of his generation, completed two full seasons in training when attributed with the wrong pedigree, not that that detracted from his obvious enthusiasm for racing – even at full stretch he always had his ears pricked.

The error dated back to 1971 when the identity of two homebred yearling fillies, belonging to the Wernhers of Someries Stud, Newmarket (now part of Sheikh Mohammed's Dalham Hall complex) got transposed after they went into training – Aglow and Rossitor were both chesnut grand-daughters of the mare, Sonsa, but one had three white legs and the other had one!

In the 1970s Pulborough trainer Guy Harwood (father of Amanda Perrett) and James Delahooke of Adstock Manor Stud in Buckinghamshire, joined forces to buy a bevy of yearling bargains and Kalaglow was one of them. They paid 11,500 guineas for the grey when he was consigned from Someries Stud (attributed with the wrong dam in the catalogue) and by the conclusion of his racing career he had earned over £250,000 and been syndicated for £5m.

Undefeated in five starts as a juvenile culminating with the Horris Hill Stakes, his three-year-old career was curtailed by a serious leg injury, sustained in the Derby, which necessitated pin-firing, a procedure far more common with jumpers than flat horses. Following a ten months' absence from the racecourse, he won the Earl of Sefton Stakes at the Craven Meeting on his reappearance as a four-year-old.

Thereafter Kalaglow went from strength to strength winning the Brigadier Gerard Stakes, before landing two of the summer's most prestigious events, the Eclipse Stakes and the King George VI and Queen Elizabeth Stakes. He was the first grey to prevail in the Ascot spectacular and the only other to succeed has been Daylami. On his finale he was unplaced in the Champion Stakes, but there was compensation for James Delahooke as the winner, Time Charter, had been bred and raised on his own stud.

Retired to stand at David Harris' recently acquired Brook Stud, Cheveley, where he remained for eleven seasons, Kalaglow was then exported to Germany; he died there in 1994. Inbred 3 x 4 to that noted grey, Palestine, he was less successful as a stallion than one might have anticipated. One of his sons, Jeune, has done well both on the racecourse and at stud in Australia.

Convinced that Kalaglow never got the quality of mares at stud here that he deserved, Guy Harwood says, "He was a very interesting horse to train, full of nervous energy, quiet as a lamb at home, but a tiger on the racecourse. The first time he ran he broke the arm of my travelling head, Frank Walker, and latterly I always took another horse with him to the races who knew him. Strange horses excited him and the adrenalin really used to run when he went racing. He produced much greater ability on the track than we saw at home."

KRIBENSIS

Grey, 1984, by Henbit - Aquaria

Owner: Sheikh Mohammed
Trainer: Sir Michael Stoute
Jockey: Richard Dunwoody
Breeder: Martin Ryan

When Kribensis, who is named after a tropical fish found in West Africa, won the 1990 Champion Hurdle convincingly as a six-year-old in course record time, he looked set to emulate other multiple winners over the two previous decades, Bula, Comedy of Errors, Night Nurse, Monksfield, Sea Pigeon and See You Then.

That victory at Prestbury Park by three lengths over the entire, Nomadic Way, who was runner-up again the following year, proved his tenth and final victory over hurdles. His only previous defeat over timber had been when unplaced as a short-priced favourite for the 1989 Champion Hurdle behind Beech Road.

On his first appearance at the festival meeting Kribensis had won the 1988 Triumph Hurdle. Apart from his first attempt at the Champion, he set up an impressive sequence of victories, which also included two Christmas Hurdles at Kempton Park, the Fighting Fifth Hurdle at Newcastle, the Gerry Feilden Hurdle at Newbury and the Kingwell Hurdle at Wincanton.

These were not the sort of races that usually concern either his trainer, Sir Michael Stoute, or his owner, Sheikh Mohammed. In the normal course of events the grey son of Derby winner, Henbit, would have been offered at the horses-in-training sale at

Newmarket at the conclusion of his three-year-old career. By then he had won three flat races and finished third in the King George V Handicap at Royal Ascot.

In December 1990 Michael Stoute announced that his grey had been breaking blood-vessels and would have to miss the season, and in fact he never ran again. One of few winners of the Triumph Hurdle to enhance his reputation subsequently – the grey Baron Blakeney was another to do so – Kribensis, who had cost Sheikh Mohammed a substantial 125,000 guineas as a foal at the Newmarket December Sales, then became Michael Stoute's hack, but not for long.

After a spell hunting in Leicestershire, he returned to Freemason Lodge stables where he became a regular conveyance for Michael Stoute's head lad, Stuart Messenger. And when any of the lads return from a seaside meeting they always bring him back a stick of rock. "He likes a variety of flavours," says Michael, "but aniseed is his favourite, closely followed by mint."

In August 2003, Kribensis paid a rather special visit to the local July Course when leading the runners round the paddock for the Grey Horse Handicap, the inaugural race in Britain confined to horses of this striking colour. But he has not always been a model of decorum. Indeed he has been a gelding since his two-year-old days – once out with the string he actually mounted the horse in front of him, much to the consternation of all concerned.

MAHMOUD

Grey, 1933, by Blenheim - Mah Mahal

Owner: H.H. Aga Khan III
Trainer: Frank Butters
Jockey: Charlie Smirke
Breeder: H.H. Aga Khan III

Karim Aga Khan's grandfather would give serious consideration whether to tip his caddy two shillings or half a crown – on the other side of the coin, although reputed to be one of the world's richest men, he was not averse to selling his Derby winners abroad, much to the dismay of breeders at home.

The Imam (spiritual leader) of the Ismaili sect of Shia Muslims, he said he would never sell his Triple Crown hero, Bahram, but he did, having previously sold both Blenheim and his son, Mahmoud. Indeed he sold Blenheim to the U.S.A. the very month after Mahmoud won the Derby in a (hand-timed) record of 2min 33.8 secs. that was only bettered by Lammtarra in 1995 – the prevailing firm ground suited the light actioned grey admirably.

A grandson of Mumtaz Mahal, from whom he inherited his light grey coat, Mahmoud was bred by his owner in France; he had actually failed to reach his reserve when offered for sale as a yearling at Deauville. Standing just 15.3 hands, he was a very elegant individual much in the mould of an Arab, with the characteristic slightly dished head.

A smart two-year-old when he won the Richmond Stakes and Champagne Stakes, he ran in all three classics, his three lengths'

Derby victory over his owner's more fancied Taj Akbar being sandwiched between a short head defeat by Pay Up in the Two Thousand Guineas, and third place behind Boswell in the St. Leger.

It is not inconceivable that with a bit of luck the attractive grey might have emulated his owner's Bahram, who had won the Triple Crown the previous year, for he lost ground at the start at Newmarket while his preparation for the oldest classic was interrupted by an attack of heel-bug.

Mahmoud completed four seasons at Egerton House Stud, Newmarket, before his sale for $84,000 (£20,000) to C.V. Whitney Farm in Kentucky. At this early stage of the war, his owner-breeder was resident in neutral Switzerland. Reputed to be suffering from a serious glandular condition, he said it was a matter of Hobson's choice – he had no funds available there and needed money to support his family.

Previously Egerton House was presided over by Richard Marsh, who trained three Derby winners there for King Edward VII, Persimmon, Diamond Jubilee and Minoru; it has now reverted to being a training establishment with soon to be retired David Loder at the helm. In the interim the Macdonald-Buchanans had run Egerton Stud in conjunction with their Lordship Stud on the opposite side of the Cambridge Road.

Mahmoud was found dead in his paddock at C.V. Whitney Farm in 1962 aged twenty-nine – he went on covering until he was twenty-five. Champion sire in the USA in 1946, where he was also a champion broodmare sire, his sons and daughters made an enormous contribution to the *American Stud Book*. One of his legacies in Europe was as maternal grandsire of his breeder's 1948 English and Irish Oaks heroine, Masaka.

MIGOLI

Grey, 1944, by Bois Roussel - Mah Iran

Owner: H.H. Aga Khan III
Trainer: Frank Butters
Jockeys: Charlie Smirke, Sir Gordon Richards
Breeder: H.H. Aga Khan III

Just four greys have won the Prix de l'Arc de Triomphe since the inaugural running in 1920, Biribi (1926), Migoli (1948), Sagamix (1998), and Dalakhani (2003). Of that quartet, both Migoli and Dalakhani carried the Aga Khan colours, but only Migoli was trained outside France.

In the post-war period there was tremendous rivalry between English and French-trained runners and this was personified by the two dominant owner-breeders on the Turf at that time, the Aga Khan, most of whose horses were then trained by Frank Butters at Newmarket, and French textile magnate, Marcel Boussac.

After winning the Dewhurst Stakes when he upset the odds laid on Boussac's Sandjar, Migoli ran eight times in each of the next two seasons. As a three-year-old he gained a memorable victory over the same owner's Nirgal in the Champion Stakes as well as defeating the odds-on favourite, Tudor Minstrel, for the Eclipse Stakes. He was also runner-up to the French invader, Pearl Diver, in the Derby, when slowly away, and third in the St. Leger to Sayajirao.

Two of Marcel Boussac's five-year-old entires, Goyama and Nirgal, provided strong opposition to Migoli as a four-year-old and he was runner-up to the former in the Coronation Cup, beaten a neck. On balance Migoli did not look as good at four as he had the preceding season. That is until the 'Arc, when he gained a famous victory over Nirgal in Goyama's enforced absence.

In all but three of his eleven victories, Migoli was ridden by Gordon Richards, but in both the Eclipse Stakes, when Gordon was claimed for Tudor Minstrel, and in the 'Arc, he was partnered by Charlie Smirke, who had already ridden one Derby winner for the Aga with Mahmoud and was to win another with Tulyar.

Initially Migoli retired to stand as a syndicated stallion at Barton Stud, Bury St. Edmunds, where his owner-breeder had stood Nasrullah for one season. He was then transferred to New England Stud, Newmarket, before following Nasrullah across the Atlantic – the grey was exported in 1959, two years after his son, Gallant Man, had triumphed in the Belmont Stakes.

Gallant Man was yet another success for Aga Khan bloodlines as Mumtaz Begum's daughter, Mah Mahal, was not only the grandam of his sire, Migoli, but she was also the dam of his maternal grandsire, Mahmoud. In fact Gallant Man had been bred by the Aga Khan and Prince Aly Khan and was one of a group of yearlings that Gallant Man's owner, Ralph Lowe, procured from them in a deal brokered by the British Bloodstock Agency.

Migoli was bought by a group of breeders headed by Donald Brokaw and went to stand at his San Juan Capistrano Ranch in California in which state the grey died, aged nineteen, towards the close of the 1963 breeding season. Overall his stud career was hardly on a par with either his distinguished racing career or his illustrious pedigree – he was an own-brother to Star of Iran, the dam of Petite Etoile.

MR. JINKS

Grey, 1926, by Tetratema - False Piety

Owner: Dermot McCalmont
Trainer: Atty Persse
Jockey: Harry Beasley
Breeder: Dermot McCalmont

When Mr. Jinks retired to stand at Dermot McCalmont's Ballylinch Stud, Co. Kilkenny, in Ireland, he was following in the footsteps of his grey forebears, his sire, Tetratema, and his grandsire, The Tetrarch; all three were trained by Dermot's cousin, Atty Persse.

Both Mr. Jinks and Tetratema were multiple juvenile winners, before gaining their most important single victory in the Two Thousand Guineas. Subsequently they demonstrated their inability to stay further, but whereas Mr. Jinks proved himself a miler, Tetratema was then campaigned exclusively as a sprinter.

With victories in the New Stakes, Royal Ascot (on his début) and July Stakes, Mr. Jinks was rated second on the Two-Year-Old Free Handicap to Tetratema's daughter, Tiffin, to whom he had finished runner-up in the National Breeders' Produce Stakes. His lack of stamina was exposed in the Derby (for which he was the unplaced favourite) and the St. Leger, while a convincing three lengths victory in the St James's Palace Stakes showed a mile was more his metier.

Mr. Jinks joined Tetratema at their owner's Ballylinch Stud, where both horses embarked up their stallion careers at a covering fee of 300 guineas. Initially he did commendably well,

GREY MAGIC

Above: Daylami. Never quite received the public recognition he deserved

Right: Abernant. 'The fastest I ever trained' Sir Noel Murless

Below: Airborne. An appropriately named winner of the 1946 Derby

Left: Alborada. Her owner-breeder's 'little grey pearl'

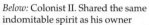

Below: Colonist II. Shared the same indomitable spirit as his owner

Below: Desert Orchid. Forged a new word in the English language, 'Dessiemania'

GREY MAGIC

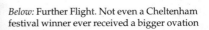

Left: Nicolaus Silver. The only grey to win the Grand National during the 20th century

Below: Further Flight. Not even a Cheltenham festival winner ever received a bigger ovation

Below: Hula Dancer. She certainly danced her way to classic victory

GREY MAGIC

Left: Grey Sovereign. A bit of a lad both on and off the racecourse

Above: Mahmoud. So long holder of the record time for the Derby

Right: Humble Duty. Demonstrated her ability against the best colts of her generation

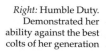

Mumtaz Mahal. Mumty or the 'flying filly', as she was known affectionately

Below: Petite Etoile. One of the biggest stars of all despite her name

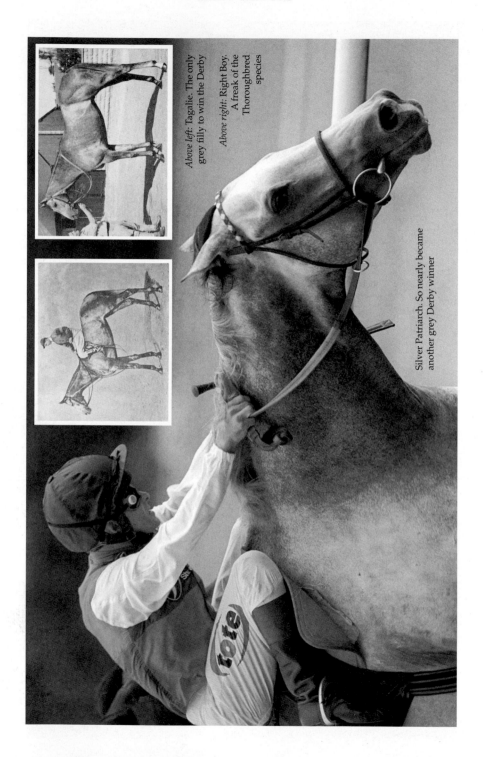

Above left: Tagalie. The only grey filly to win the Derby

Above right: Right Boy. A freak of the Thoroughbred species

Silver Patriarch. So nearly became another grey Derby winner

Above: Rooster Booster. One of the most popular grey jumpers of his generation

Below: Tetratema. A chip off the old block both on the racecourse and at stud

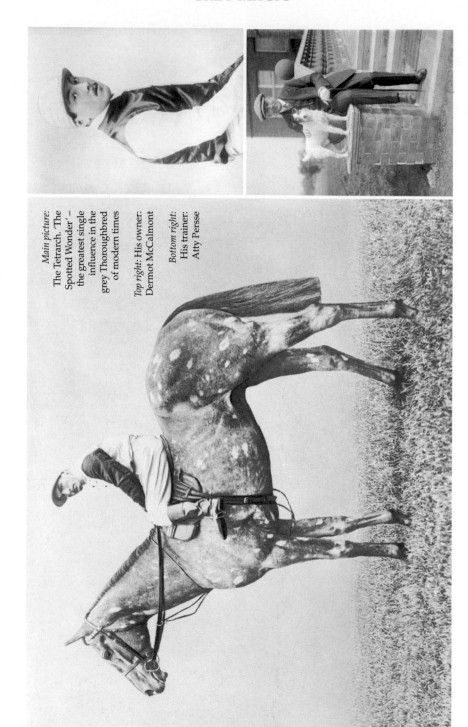

Main picture:
The Tetrarch. 'The
Spotted Wonder' –
the greatest single
influence in the
grey Thoroughbred
of modern times

Top right: His owner:
Dermot McCalmont

Bottom right:
His trainer:
Atty Persse

but most of his stock reflected his own shortcomings; they made their mark as two-year-olds only to demonstrate decided stamina limitations in later life.

By the time of his death in 1952 aged twenty-six, Mr. Jinks had been all but forgotten by flat breeders. However, in the three previous years he featured as the maternal grandsire of the triple Champion Hurdle winner, Hatton's Grace. During the same period, Vincent O'Brien's versatile gelding also brought off a big handicap double on the flat in the Irish Lincolnshire and Irish Cesarewitch.

There is another link with jump racing in Ireland as Mr. Jinks was ridden in all his races by Atty Persse's stable jockey, Harry Beasley, whose son, Bobby, partnered the grey Nicolaus Silver to victory in the 1961 Grand National. A few months later came the much publicised 'Christine Keeler affair' and the resignation of War Minister, John Profumo – his wife, the former film star, Valerie Hobson, was Bobby Beasley's aunt.

MUMTAZ MAHAL

Grey, 1921, by The Tetrarch - Lady Josephine

Owner: H.H. Aga Khan III
Trainer: Dick Dawson
Jockeys: George Hulme, George Archibald
Breeder: Lady Sykes

Mumtaz Mahal, named after the Indian princess for whom the world's most famous mausoleum, the Taj Mahal, was built, was a star of the sales ring, on the racecourse, where she earned the soubriquet, 'The Flying Filly' and at stud – her worldwide influence in breeding terms cannot be overstated.

In the early 1920s George Lambton laid the foundations of the old Aga Khan's bloodstock empire by purchasing a number of yearling fillies. At Tattersalls' September Yearling Sales of 1922 in the old Glasgow Paddocks at Doncaster he paid 9,100 guineas for a daughter of The Tetrarch and leading juvenile, Lady Josephine, one of seventeen yearlings consigned by Lady Sykes from her famous Sledmere Stud in the old East Riding of Yorkshire. This was the highest auction price for a filly since 1900 when Sceptre realised 10,000 guineas as a yearling.

"I thought her one of the best animals I ever saw in my life," said George Lambton. And a report in that year's *Bloodstock Breeders' Review* concurred, "As an individual she is wonderful, as near perfection as imagination can conceive. Her conformation is ideal and she has both size and quality. This does not necessarily mean she is bound to be a racing paragon."

It was upon George Lambton's recommendation that the Aga Khan appointed Dick Dawson to train for him at Whatcombe, near Wantage (the yard now occupied by Ruby Tiger's trainer,

Paul Cole), and it was not long before he too was enamoured with the grey filly, now called Mumtaz Mahal.

For her final gallop before her racing début at Newmarket, Mumtaz Mahal was set to give 28lbs to Friar's Daughter, who had already scored convincingly on her first public appearance, but the grey beat her rival by over a hundred yards. "I was so astounded and excited that I nearly fell off my hack. I had no idea that she was such a wonder," Dick Dawson related afterwards.

Had he possessed a crystal ball he would have been equally astonished by the fact that Friar's Daughter and Mumtaz Mahal were to become the dam and grandam respectively of the Aga Khan's second and third Derby winners, Bahram (1935) and Mahmoud (1936), the latter a striking grey. Blandford, the sire of Bahram and the grandsire of Mahmoud, is buried at Whatcombe.

It soon transpired that Mumtaz Mahal was no morning glory as she proved herself in no uncertain fashion on the racecourse. Having justified favouritism at the first time of asking, she then won the Queen Mary Stakes (by ten lengths), National Breeders' Produce Stakes (by four lengths), Molecomb Stakes (by ten lengths), and Champagne Stakes (by three lengths). All were at prohibitive odds and most were only small fields as she simply frightened off the opposition.

However, on her finale that season in the Imperial Produce Plate at Kempton Park, a combination of factors brought about her downfall. Although she had not been quite herself, her trainer decided to let her take her chance despite a torrential two-hour downpour before the race which made the ground unsuitably holding for such a good actioned filly – and she was beaten half a length.

Notwithstanding this reversal, Mumty, as she was known affectionately, was rated the champion two-year-old of her generation, and was now referred to as 'The Flying Filly'. Sent for a few months' winter holiday to Highclere Stud, on the other side of Newbury, owned by Dick Dawson's enthusiastic patron, Lord Carnarvon, she was turned out daily to enjoy a change of scenery.

There was always going to be speculation with such a fast juvenile not only whether she would train on, but also whether she would stay. Her stamina appeared suspect when she was second, beaten a length-and-a-half by Plack as favourite for the One Thousand Guineas on her seasonal reappearance after looking to have an unassailable lead at the Bushes. Those fears were confirmed when she was fifth of seven in the Coronation Stakes.

That was the only time she finished out of the first two and, after Royal Ascot, she reverted to her true metier of sprinting, winning the King George Stakes and the Nunthorpe Stakes, by a commanding six lengths. By the close of her career many people regarded her as the fastest performer ever seen on a racecourse, faster even than her illustrious sire, The Tetrarch, from whom she inherited her spotted coat.

Although none of Mumtaz Mahal's own progeny proved as talented on the racecourse, two of her daughters changed the content of the world's stud books. They were Mah Mahal, whose sire, Gainsborough, stood next door to Highclere at Harwood Stud (now Gainsborough Stud), and Mumtaz Begum; her sire, Blenheim, was bred at Highclere and was the Aga Khan's first Derby winner.

Just to give a flavour of their enormous contribution, mention should be made of some of their classic winning descendants. From Mah Mahal come Mahmoud (Derby), Petite Etoile (1000 Guineas, Oaks), Nishapour (French 2000 Guineas), and Zainta (French Oaks), as well as the disqualified Oaks 'winner', Aliysa – the latter is the grandam of Alamshar (2003 Irish Derby, King George VI and Queen Elizabeth Diamond Stakes).

Amongst those tracing to Mumtaz Begum are Shergar (Derby), Oh So Sharp (1000 Guineas, Oaks, St. Leger), Shantou (St. Leger), Ginetta (French 1000 Guineas), and Kalamoun (French 2000 Guineas). Of these classic winners, Mahmoud, Petite Etoile, Nishapour and Kalamoun were greys bred by the Aga Khan Studs. Also from Mumtaz Mahal come Nasrullah, one of the world's most influential sires, his three-parts brother, Royal

Charger, and the greys Abernant and Migoli.

It was not very expedient timing when in 1938, after producing four foals at his stud in Ireland, the Aga Khan sent Mumtaz Mahal to his French stud at Marly-la-Ville, about twenty miles from Paris. In due course the Germans seized Haras de Marly-la-Ville and the majority of the occupants, but, for whatever reason, Mumtaz Mahal was not taken and she died there just after the war.

Like so many exceptional fillies, Mumtaz Mahal had a mind of her own. That great stud master, Peter Burrell, recalled seeing her at Goodwood before the Molecomb Stakes, a match which she won at odds of 40-1 on. "She looked magnificent, and would have passed as a three-year-old. She was very much on her toes in the paddock, the layout of which was a single rail, which separated the horses from the spectators. As the filly turned a corner she lashed out at a man leaning on the rail and smashed his arm."

Whilst in training at Whatcombe, the Flying Filly, always idiosyncratic, formed an attachment with a gelding called Lakers, and he accompanied her whenever she went to the races. By the time she was a broodmare she had developed a contrasting dislike of cattle and woe betide any unfortunate bullock that happened to be turned out in the same paddock!

MYROBELLA

Grey, 1930, by Tetratema - Dolabella

Lessee: 5th Earl of Lonsdale
Trainer: Fred Darling
Jockey: Sir Gordon Richards
Breeder: National Stud

When William Hall-Walker (later Lord Wavertree), whose brewing family presented the Walker Art Gallery to the City of Liverpool, gave his stud at Tully in Ireland to the British nation in 1916, the forty-three broodmares included Dolabella. In 1943 the breeding operation was transferred to Lord Furness' Compton Stud at Gillingham in Dorset, and Dolabella's daughter, Myrobella, was one of the mares to cross the Irish Sea.

While Gondolette, the dam of Dolabella, became a great foundation mare for the 17th Lord Derby (she is the third dam of Hyperion), Dolabella did likewise for the National Stud and Myrobella proved to be her key offspring. Trained by Fred Darling, she was leased for the duration of her racing career to the 5th Lord Lonsdale, an arrangement organised by the National Stud's long serving director, Peter Burrell.

In his memoirs, *Old Sportsmen Never Die*, Peter Burrell recalls, "Fred Darling, who trained for us at Beckhampton, told me he couldn't take more than two yearlings to train for Lord Lonsdale as the latter seldom paid his training bills and owed Darling a lot of money. Lord Lonsdale's extravagant way of living was proverbial and the day had arrived when his trustees had to put him on an allowance to control him and save him from bankruptcy. His butler had not been paid for years until Myrobella won at Ascot!"

That victory came in the Fern Hill Stakes as a three-year-old, when she also won the King George Stakes and Challenge Stakes; in addition she was beaten a short head for the Nunthorpe Stakes and finished third in the One Thousand Guineas. The preceding year she had won her last five starts, including the National Breeders' Produce Stakes and Champagne Stakes by an aggregate of eleven lengths. She headed the Free Handicap, the only time on record that fillies have ranked first, second and third.

Myrobella brought considerable honour and glory to the National Stud as a broodmare, her outstanding offspring being Big Game. Leased for the duration of his racing career to King George VI, he won the New Two Thousand Guineas and Champion Stakes of 1942, prior to becoming a champion sire of broodmares for the National Stud.

Big Game's prowess as a sire of fillies soon became manifest and his first crop of two-year-olds in 1946 provided all four runners in that season's Molecomb Stakes, but it was no easier to find the winner with the outsider of the quartet prevailing at 33-1!

Considering that Lord Wavertree, the man who inspired the old Aga Khan to take up racing and breeding, based all his matings on the signs of the zodiac, he left a tremendous legacy for the National Stud.

For her part, Myrobella also produced Snowberry, the dam of Chamossaire (1945 St Leger), who was also bred there; Snowberry is also the third dam of Snow Knight (1974 Derby). However, none of these descendants of Myrobella were greys.

MYSTIKO

Grey, 1988, by Secreto - Caracciola

Owner: Marcia, Lady Beaverbrook
Trainer: Clive Brittain
Jockey: Michael Roberts
Breeder: Kingston Park Stud Inc.

Visitors to Newmarket in May, 1991, witnessed an astonishing classic double for greys when Shadayid won the One Thousand Guineas and Mystiko won the Two Thousand Guineas, both of them bred and conceived in America.

That season at Newmarket, Lady Beaverbrook's grey Mystiko laid claims to being one of the best 7 to 8 furlong performers of his generation, his Guineas triumph being sandwiched between facile victories in the European Free Handicap and the Challenge Stakes – all three victories were recorded on the wide open expanse of the Rowley Course. That was far in advance of anything he had achieved as a two-year-old, or anything that he would achieve at four years.

Two people closely involved with the front running Mystiko behind the scenes were Joss Collins of the British Bloodstock Agency, who bought the light grey colt as a yearling on behalf of Lady Beaverbrook at the Keeneland Select Sale in July 1989 for $150,000, and his father-in-law, Bob Crowhurst.

Owner of Crockfords Stud opposite Tattersalls' Solario Yard on the Woodditton Road, Bob Crowhurst was one of Newmarket's most eminent veterinary surgeons. He was also one of Lady B's key advisers and one of her best homebred winners,

Easter Sun, was bred and reared at Crockfords. Remarkably the stud bred two grey winners of the Queen Mary Stakes in Grizel (by Grey Sovereign), and Rory's Rocket (by Roan Rocket).

Mystiko had been consigned as a yearling by Kingston Park Stud Incorporated, which represented the Kentucky branch of David Hains' Kingston Park Stud in Australia. A couple of the champions he has bred there are Rose of Kingston and Lowan Star – Claude, their respective sire and maternal grandsire, belong to the same female family as Mystiko.

It is fascinating to speculate what this grey classic winner would have achieved had he been placed with Lady Beaverbrook's other principal trainer, Dick Hern, at West Ilsley instead of Clive Brittain as this notably highly strung individual performed so much better at Newmarket than anywhere else. That was attributed, at least in part, to his being a bad traveller. Clive Brittain also had the advantage of swimming facilities for his horses.

Modern breeders would always favour a Guineas winner over a St. Leger winner, yet it was Lady Beaverbrook's Bustino who made his mark as a sire and not Mystiko. Based at Barton Stud, Bury St. Edmunds, he stood alongside two more of his owner's horses, Terimon, another grey, and Charmer. With dwindling support, Mystiko was eventually exported to Italy where his relative, Claude, originated, but he never acclimatised there and returned to England where he was put down shortly afterwards.

It was Lord Rosebery, owner-breeder of the grey Oaks heroine, Sleeping Partner, who encouraged Marcia Beaverbrook to take up racing in the mid-1960s following the death of her husband – he was the breeder of Miracle, who won the Eclipse Stakes for Rosebery, and that was the name she gave to one of her first significant winners.

NICER

Grey, 1990, by Pennine Walk - Everything Nice

Owner: The Hon. Mrs. Catherine Corbett
Trainer: Barry Hills
Jockey: Michael Hills
Breeder: Barronstown Bloodstock Ltd.

With a predilection for grey fillies, Catherine Corbett, from Coates, near Cirencester, in Gloucestershire, is a long standing owner of Barry Hills' stable. She is also a sister of Robert Acton, who manages Klaus Jacobs' Newsells Park Stud in Hertfordshire and sister-in-law of her former trainer, the late Atty Corbett, uncle to Californian trainer, Ben Cecil.

In 1983 Mrs Corbett's colours of royal blue, silver striped sleeves, red hooped cap, were carried to victory by Desirable in the Cheveley Park Stakes and in 1989 her Negligent won the Rockfel Stakes. Both greys went on to finish third in the One Thousand Guineas before being entered in Barry Hills' annual consignment at the Newmarket December Sales.

Desirable was purchased by Coolmore for £1m guineas, which was just one bid (20,000 guineas) short of the record set by Tenea two years before, while Negligent was withdrawn from the 1990 sale having been bought privately beforehand by Sheikh Mohammed.

Both Desirable and Negligent had been yearling purchases and so too was Nicer. Another grey filly bred in Ireland, Nicer had first been sold as a foal by David Nagle's Barronstown Stud, Co. Wicklow, for 16,500 guineas to John Johnson of Bishop Wilton

Stud in the old East Riding of Yorkshire. Lord Halifax's stud groom at Garrowby, he then sold her for 27,000 guineas at the following year's Newmarket October Yearling Sales when consigned from Hamish Alexander's Partridge Close Stud, Co. Durham.

In fact Catherine Corbett owned Nicer in partnership with her Cotswolds' neighbour, Christopher Wright of Chrysalis Records and owner of Stratford Place Stud. "Chris is a friend and plays tennis with my husband, so when we discovered that we both wanted Nicer we decided to share her," she explained.

On two-year-old form, there was little to suggest that Nicer would achieve classic compensation for the two third places that Desirable and Negligent had achieved in the Guineas. But following a successful reappearance in the Masaka Stakes, Kempton Park, the Pennine Walk filly triumphed in the Irish equivalent at the Curragh, scoring by two lengths in the hands of her trainer's twin son, Michael Hills.

At that year's Newmarket December Sales, Nicer was purchased by Fahd Salman of Newgate Stud for 270,000 guineas, and joined Neil Drysdale in California. She was carrying only her second foal when she was bought by the Lloyd-Webbers' Watership Down Stud at Kingsclere in Hampshire at the 1996 Keeneland Breeding Stock Sale in November, carrying to Diesis. She was later sold to Japan.

Catherine Corbett's love of racing in general and greys in particular goes back a long way, right back to the afternoon when, as a six-year-old, she backed a 33-1 winner, Gipsy Grey, in a point-to-point. Her involvement has not just been on the flat as she also owned a smart grey 'chaser during the 1990s in Morceli.

NICOLAUS SILVER

Grey, 1952, by Nicolaus - Rays of Montrose

Owner: Jeremy Vaughan
Trainer: Fred Rimell
Jockey: Bobby Beasley
Breeder: James Heffernan

When outsider Nicolaus Silver, partnered by Bobby Beasley, won the 1961 Grand National, he became only the second grey to score at Aintree since The Lamb gained the second of his two 'National triumphs ninety years earlier. He was also the second of Fred Rimell's four 'National winners along with ESB, Gay Trip and Rag Trade.

Most people were unaware of the considerable drama that preceded Nicolaus Silver's great Aintree success. At the time there was a gang of dopers doing the rounds and his trainer took the precaution of putting another grey in Nicolaus Silver's box at his Kinnersley stables in Worcestershire. Sure enough, the substitute grey, High Spot, was 'got at' and he was so badly affected that he never ran again.

Skulduggery was afoot. On the Wednesday before the 'National, Alex Bird found one of the bookmaking fraternity offering 40-1 Nicolaus Silver, while none of their rivals had him priced above 28-1. He promptly had £10,000 to £250. Later the professional backer reported that it was the only time that this particular firm had accepted a significant telephone wager from him without the clerk referring the transaction to higher authority.

There had been another scare a few days before the race when it was discovered that Nicolaus Silver had a very swollen leg as the result of being pricked by the farrier. The Rimells stayed up all night applying poultices and gradually the swelling subsided, but it meant that the gelding missed a final and crucial piece of work; indeed his participation was in doubt on the very morning of the race.

The grey had been bred in Ireland by James Heffernan of Cuckoo Hill, Cahir, Co. Tipperary. But when he failed to make his modest reserve of 300 guineas at the 1953 Newmarket October Yearling Sales, he returned home, was immediately gelded and turned out before being broken in and hunted with the Tipperary hounds.

A natural jumper, who never had to be schooled as a youngster, he was initially put into training by his Irish owner-breeder with Dan Kirwan, from Gowran in Co. Kilkenny. Twice sold on to different patrons of the stable, he then came up for sale after his trainer was killed in a car accident. As an eight-year-old he was secured for 2,600 guineas at Goffs' Ballsbridge Sales in November 1960 for Jeremy Vaughan.

Much of he credit for buying him was due to Fred Rimell's wife, Mercy, who rode the grey in all his work prior to Aintree. She remembers, "Jeremy was very keen to win the 'National as his father, Douglas, had owned the 1948 runner-up, First of the Dandies. We went to the sale with Jeremy and bought him for Jeremy's limit; Ivor Herbert was underbidder. The only one of two horses catalogued who were qualified for the 'National, he was the most beautiful looking horse who would have won any light-weight hunter class. But the key to him was the going – he had to have top of the ground."

If any rider was qualified to ride in the 'National it was surely Bobby Beasley, who also won a Gold Cup on Roddy Owen and a Champion Hurdle on Another Flash. His grandfather, Harry (at eighty-five, the oldest man ever to ride a winner), won the 1891 'National on Come Away and he and three of his brothers all rode together in the 1879 'National – the eldest, Tommy, rode three 'National winners in the 1880s. Just for good measure Bobby Jnr's father-in-law, Arthur Thompson, rode two post-war 'National winners for Neville Crump, Sheila's Cottage and Teal.

Bobby Beasley, the son of Atty Persse's stable jockey, another Harry, who rode the grey Mr. Jinks, had first seen Nicolaus Silver when he won a three-mile 'chase at Naas. "Later he came to Fred Rimell, but he was very stuffy," he recalled. "He was a glutton and would even eat his own bedding. They had to put down peat moss for him to lie on. Because he was so gross he was very difficult to get fully fit. But Nicolaus Silver had won the Kim Muir 'Chase at the Cheltenham festival just seventeen days before he won the Grand National."

Many 'National winners tend to lose their way after the unique demands of Liverpool, but three weeks later Nicolaus Silver was runner-up in the Whitbread Gold Cup. The following season he returned to Aintree to win the Grand Sefton 'Chase as well as landing the Great Yorkshire 'Chase at Doncaster. However, he was unplaced in the next two 'Nationals, albeit he completed the course each time, finishing seventh in 1962 and tenth in 1963 – on both occasions the going was on the soft side.

In between he had been consigned to Botterills' December Sales at Ascot where the ten-year-old was retained by Fred Rimell for 3,500 guineas acting on behalf of property magnate, Bernard Sunley. His colours had been carried into third place by Clear Profit in the 1960 'National behind Merryman II – it was Nicolaus Silver who had deprived Merryman of a second successive victory at Aintree the following year.

Although Nicolaus Silver retired with a reputation for breaking blood-vessels, he was frequently seen out hunting with the Whaddon 'Chase – when Bernard Sunley died in November 1964 the grey passed to his daughter, Joan Tice. Considering that he had negotiated all those formidable 'National fences, it was ironic that he should have to be put down after breaking a leg out drag-hunting at Chartwell in Kent.

By the law of averages another grey Grand National winner is long overdue, albeit two have come very close to emulating Nicolaus Silver in recent times. Suny Bay finished runner-up in 1997 and 1998 as did What's Up Boys only four years later.

NOCTURNAL SPREE

Grey, 1972, by Supreme Sovereign - Night Attire

Owners: Anne-Hart O'Kelly & Partners
Trainer: Stuart Murless
Jockey: Johnny Roe
Breeder: Jerry Dillon

Two of the five English classics in 1975 were won by greys, but by very contrasting margins. The first of them, the One Thousand Guineas, saw Nocturnal Spree prevail by a short head, and the last of them, the St. Leger, went to Bruni by a commanding ten lengths.

Nocturnal Spree, who inherited the grey coat of her sire, the notoriously difficult to handle Supreme Sovereign, was a good filly on her day if somewhat lacking in quality. But like so many of the breed, she did not possess the soundest of limbs and suffered a split pastern at both two and three years, injuries that curtailed, and finally ended, her racing career prematurely.

In fact Stuart Murless, younger brother of Noel, only ever saddled her four times, three of those appearances being at his local Curragh course. Third in September on her solitary outing as a juvenile, she came to Newmarket with a maiden win in April under her belt, and then, after her narrow One Thousand Guineas victory, she finished a well beaten fourth in the Irish equivalent when a warm favourite partnered by Lester Piggott.

Her next public appearance was at the Newmarket December Sales where her four owners, Denis and Anne-Hart O'Kelly, Raymond Keogh and Denis Coakley, comparative newcomers to racing, received the top price of 96,000 guineas, making her the third most expensive filly ever sold in Great Britain. Bought by agent, George Blackwell, on behalf of Eddie Taylor, the world renowned Canadian breeder of Northern Dancer, she was the first One Thousand Guineas heroine to go through the ring since 1954 when Festoon made the then record of 36,000 guineas.

It proved a notable sale for greys as the Palestine horse, Capistrano, realised 50,000 guineas, which bettered the previous record for a stallion of 47,000 guineas set by Solario back at the 1932 July Sales. The partners in Nocturnal Spree were well rewarded financially as they had originally paid 6,200 guineas through Tom Cooper of the British Bloodstock Agency (Ireland), when she had been consigned to Goffs as a yearling by her breeder, Jerry Dillon, from his Newborough Stud, Co. Limerick.

Before being exported to Canada, Nocturnal Spree was covered the following spring by Bustino. The latter was bred by Edgar Cooper Bland of Rutland Stud (now owned by Sheikh Mohammed), as was Nocturnal Spree's dam, Night Attire. Both are descendants of the celebrated foundation mare, Rosetta. None of Nocturnal Spree's offspring proved of any great consequence.

Bloodstock was by no means the only sound investment that Edgar Cooper Bland made during his long life. When he died aged ninety-one in 1984, he possessed the biggest private collection of paintings by his old friend, Sir Alfred Munnings. Whenever the great sporting artist was short of funds (as he constantly was as a younger man), Cooper Bland was only too pleased to acquire one of his works for a nominal sum!

ONE MAN

Grey, 1988, by Remainder Man - Steal On

Owner: John Hales
Trainer: Gordon W. Richards
Jockeys: Richard Dunwoody, Brian Harding, Tony Dobbin
Breeder: Hugh J. Holohan

On May 10th 1993, Doncaster Bloodstock Sales held a unique dispersal of 127 horses following the death the previous year of leading National Hunt trainer, Arthur Stephenson, at his Crawleas stables at windswept Bishop Auckland in Co. Durham.

Potential purchasers came from far and wide, but One Man, the second top priced individual at 68,000 guineas, who was offered as the joint property of W.A. Stephenson & Son and Swiss-based Peter Piller, had only to cross the Pennines. Bought by Gordon Richards from Penrith on behalf of John Hales, Lot 111, a five-year-old grey gelding, had won novice hurdles at Newcastle, Nottingham and Ayr that season.

Far exceeding Hales' original budget of 30,000 guineas, he was bought to replace his owner's very first horse, The Toyman, who had been tragically killed in his very first outing. A new patron of the stable, this toys manufacturer was to hit the jackpot in his own business with the ubiquitous Teletubbies and One Man was to make his own name over fences, which had always looked to be his true metier.

In 1994 he won the Hennessy Cognac Gold Cup, followed by two successive King George VI 'Chases – actually both were staged in 1996, the first being a rearranged running at Sandown

Park in January (Kempton Park on Boxing Day had been abandoned due to the weather), while the second was back at its traditional home when he set a new course record.

A beaten favourite in the 1994 Royal & SunAlliance 'Chase and down the field in the 1996 and 1997 Gold Cups, One Man, whom his trainer always referred to as his rubber ball, bounced back in sensational fashion to win the 1998 Queen Mother Champion 'Chase over two miles as a ten-year-old.

On that occasion he produced a flawless display of jumping, indicating that his previous failures at Cheltenham were due to lack of stamina – in both Gold Cups he had floundered up the final hill after looking to hold a winning chance. Previously the cause of his disappointing runs was thought to be a tendency to break blood-vessels. However, that was of academic interest only as tragically, just over two weeks after the Champion 'Chase, he had a fatal fall, breaking a leg when bowling along in front in the Mumm Melling 'Chase over the Mildmay fences at Aintree. His record stood at an extraordinary twenty victories from thirty-six career starts.

The grey, who seemed almost a reincarnation of Desert Orchid (the horse that motivated John Hales to become an owner in the first place), has a race named after him at Wetherby, which was the favourite course of his former trainer, Arthur Stephenson. It was as a replacement for One Man that John Hales procured Mister Banjo at the Doncaster Spring Sales of 2000 for 240,000 guineas, which at that time constituted a world record for a jumper. And at the 2004 festival the same colours prevailed in the Champion 'Chase for a second time with the very talented Azertyuiop.

Like all Arthur Stephenson's top horses, One Man had originally been procured unseen from Tom Costello of Newmarket-on-Fergus, Co. Clare. The Irishman has earned a reputation second to none as a purveyor of National Hunt horses to trainers in England and Arthur was his first major customer. In his time Tom Costello has sold six individual future Cheltenham Gold Cup winners, highlighted by triple hero,

Best Mate; another was Arthur Stephenson's The Thinker.

An additional protégé was another grey, Tom Costalot (the name says it all!), trained at Stow-on-the-Wold by Susan Nock. This permit holder also had that distinguished grey front-runner, Senor El Betrutti, who gained memorable wins at Cheltenham in the Thomas Pink Gold Cup and Tripleprint Gold Cup in the same season.

PALARIVA

Grey, 1953, by Palestine - Rivaz

Owner: H.H. Aga Khan III
Trainer: Alec Head
Jockey: Roger Poincelet
Breeders: H.H. Aga Khan III, Prince Aly Khan

Although she was trained in France by Alec Head, the very speedy grey filly, Palariva, ran marginally more often in England than she did on the other side of The Channel – successful in ten of her fourteen starts, she was only once unplaced, a particularly remarkable record of consistency for a sprinter, male or female.

In each of her two seasons in training Palariva scored at Royal Ascot, winning the Chesham Stakes at two years and the King's Stand Stakes at three years. She earned a comparable record at Goodwood, unbelievably then a once-a-year meeting, winning the Molecomb Stakes and the King George Stakes. Inexplicably she was never given a rating in the Two-Year-Old Free Handicap.

In the Molecomb, which in those days was confined to fillies, she actually finished runner-up, beaten a head by La Fresnes (demoted to last place, the latter was destined to became a noted broodmare at the Norfolks' Angmering Park Stud), and she was also awarded the following season's Prix de Seine-et-Oise on the disqualification of Midget II. Both victories materialised as the result of objections lodged by her rider, Roger Poincelet.

The Seine-et-Oise represented her one and only attempt beyond 5 furlongs – in France that season she also won the Prix de Saint – Georges, Prix du Grôs-Chène, and Prix du Petit Couvert, all of them Group sprints nowadays. She won both the King's Stand Stakes and Prix de Saint-Georges in record time; at Royal Ascot, she defeated Vigo, another grey, by a short head.

A daughter of Nasrullah's own-sister, Rivaz, Palariva was an Aga Khan bred through and through – by Palestine, from whom she inherited her grey colouring, she was an early foal (January 23), and was actually born at Barton Stud, Bury St. Edmunds, when her dam was visiting the Aly Khan bred Tehran, the sire of Tulyar. Habat, another grey grandson of Palariva, also features in this book.

Palariva had another distinguished grandson in Kalamoun. Winner of the French Two Thousand Guineas in 1973 for the present Aga Khan, Kalamoun established a small dynasty of grey stallions in France through his son, Kenmare, the sire of Highest Honor and Kendor. Highest Honor retired to stud at Haras du Quesnay at Deauville, which is managed for the Head family by Alec's daughter, Martine.

PALESTINE

Grey, 1947, by Fair Trial - Una

Owner: H.H. Aga Khan III
Trainers: Frank Butters, Marcus Marsh
Jockeys: Charlie Smirke, Sir Gordon Richards
Breeders: H.H. Aga Khan III, Prince Aly Khan

Palestine inflicted the first of two classic defeats on the luckless American owned and bred Prince Simon, who started a well backed favourite for both the Two Thousand Guineas and the Derby in 1950, only to be beaten a short head at Newmarket and a head at Epsom.

The remainder of the Two Thousand Guineas field were left trailing in their wake. Five lengths away in third place was Masked Light to whom Palestine had finished runner-up in the Middle Park Stakes the previous autumn.

That was Palestine's solitary reversal in seven juvenile starts when he had won the Sandown Park Stud Produce Stakes (by four lengths), Coventry Stakes (by three lengths), National Breeders' Produce Stakes (by three lengths), Richmond Stakes (by four lengths), Gimcrack Stakes (by four lengths), and Champagne Stakes (by eight lengths). Few top two-year-olds are subjected to such a rigorous campaign.

Frank Butters had been reluctant to saddle Palestine in the Middle Park considering that he had been exploited quite enough already. Not long afterwards the trainer suffered cerebral injuries when knocked off his bicycle by a passing lorry on leaving his Fitzroy House stables (now occupied by Michael Bell, trainer of 2005 Derby winner, Motivator). Although the Aga Khan paid for him to see the top brain specialists in the world, he was forced to relinquish his licence in favour of his colleague, Marcus Marsh.

For his new trainer, Palestine won five of his six starts at three years, his Two Thousand Guineas victory being followed by the St. James's Palace Stakes and Sussex Stakes in both of which he was an odds-on favourite. There were only four runners at Goodwood, where Palestine was followed home by two more greys in Donore and Zodiac.

On his penultimate outing the Aga Khan's colt was fourth in the Eclipse Stakes, the only time he ever finished out of the first two. Like most sons of Fair Trial, whose stallion sons exerted a worldwide influence, a mile was his optimum distance.

Syndicated to stand at his owner's Gilltown Stud, Co. Kildare, Palestine remained there for a decade until interest permeated through for the stallion from Japan. As Bill McEnery of Portmarnock Stud, Co. Dublin (whose nephew, Martyn McEnery, bred Red Rum), was not keen to sell his four shares, he and the Japanese party were requested to submit sealed bids. Much to Bill's surprise his offer of just over £20,000 won the day and Portmarnock became the horse's permanent home. He died there in 1974 aged twenty-seven.

A commendably successful sire, whose sons and daughters also made their mark at stud, he is best remembered for the 1958 Two Thousand Guineas winner, Pall Mall – The Queen's first homebred classic winner, he was a chesnut despite carrying no fewer than three lines of The Tetrarch. The pick of Palestine's grey offspring to race in England was probably the Aga Khan's filly, Palariva.

One of the reasons for the success of the Aga Khan Studs over a long period has been the readiness to acquire fresh bloodlines and Palestine is a grandson of the French Oaks heroine, Uganda – the latter was procured in 1927 in a package deal following the death that January of her owner-breeder, Edouard Kann.

Always conscious of the need to replenish his breeding stock, Karim Aga Khan has enjoyed considerable success stemming from en bloc purchases of both the Boussac and Dupré studs in the 1970s. In March 2005 it was announced that he had acquired the French bloodstock empire of the Lagardere family, including the champion grey stallion, Linamix.

PASTY

Grey, 1973, by Raffingora - Ma Marie

Owner: Percival Williams
Trainer: Peter Walwyn
Jockey: Pat Eddery
Breeder: Percival Williams

Peter Walwyn trained two exceptional grey grand-daughters of Grey Sovereign in Humble Duty (by Sovereign Path) and Pasty (by Raffingora), both winners of the Lowther Stakes and the Cheveley Park Stakes.

Each was rated the leading juvenile of her sex and it is a matter of opinion as to which was superior at that age. In the respective Two-Year-Old Free Handicaps, Humble Duty was rated with 9st, while Pasty was allotted 8st 13lbs; *Timeform* assessed them in reverse order with Humble Duty on 121 and Pasty on 122.

Pasty's victory in the Lowther Stakes on the opening day of the York Ebor Meeting provided her owner-breeder, Percival Williams, from Kings Caple in Herefordshire, with a sensational double as May Hill, his only other filly in training that season, triumphed in the Yorkshire Oaks. It also provided immediate compensation to their trainer who had just witnessed the great Grundy defeated at odds-on for the Benson & Hedges Gold Cup (now Juddmonte International).

Unlike Humble Duty, Pasty did not train on as a three-year-old, but she was unbeaten in five juvenile outings – she started off at lowly Wolverhampton and Peter Walwyn admitted to not having any idea initially just how good she was. But he would have known that her dam, Ma Marie, had been trained by Humphrey Cottrill, whose father, Harry, once presided over his famous Seven Barrows training stable outside Lambourn.

Percival Williams had procured Ma Marie, already named, as a yearling from Sir Victor Sassoon's Eve Stud at the 1957 Newmarket First October Sales for 1,400 guineas. Eve Stud (later called Woodditton Stud and now owned by Sheikh Mohammed) was a name derived from Sassoon's initials, E.V. (Ellice Victor). As a two-year-old she won the £1,000 Princess Stakes, the race immediately after the July Cup won by the grey Right Boy.

Percival Williams, whose ancestors originated in Cornwall (hence the name, Pasty) where their fortune accrued from tin mining, was master and huntsman of the local Four Burrow Hunt for over forty years. He is also the grandfather of Venetia Williams, who trains at Aramstone (see Teeton Mill), the family farm in Herefordshire where her father, John, still keeps a few broodmares and John's cousin, Richard, owns and manages Scorrier House Stud at Redruth in Cornwall where he bred the recent Group 1 winner, Firebreak.

Neither Humble Duty nor Pasty had protracted stud careers and the few foals they had were of little account. In fact Pasty was retired from the Aramstone paddocks after producing a colt by one Gold Cup winner in Ragstone and a filly by another in Sagaro, which may not have been the most inspired of matings.

PELTING

Grey, 1958, by Vilmorin - Firmament

Owner: Dawn Wigan
Trainer: Arthur Budgett
Jockey: Stan Clayton
Breeder: Charles W. Gordon

On the traditional first Wednesday in June, Derby Day on Epsom Downs used to open with the Stewards' Handicap over 5 furlongs. With top of the ground conditions and a following wind, the initial downhill gradient makes this the fastest course in the country – when Indigenous scored in 1960 the time of 53.6 secs (about 42 mph) constituted a world record time for the distance.

Two fillies featured in *Grey Magic*, Pelting and Caterina, also won the Stewards' Handicap during the 1960s and the former became an exceptional foundation mare for Dawn and Dare Wigan of West Blagdon, near Cranborne, in Dorset – she had inherited the filly as a yearling in 1959 upon the death of her father, Charles Gordon.

Although she was by the sprinter, Vilmorin, who sired another outstanding grey broodmare in Jojo, Pelting had classic antecedents as her first three dams, Firmament (by Windsor Lad), Guiding Star (by Papyrus), and Ocean Light (by Sunstar) were all by Derby winners. Both Ocean Light's parents were homebred classic winners at Epsom for Jack Joel as Sunstar won the 1911 Derby and Glass Doll won the 1907 Oaks.

A cousin of fellow bloodstock agent, Charlie Gordon-Watson,

Dawn Wigan's son, James, who runs London Thoroughbred Services from Biddlesgate Farm, one of the original farms that comprised their grandfather's Boveridge Park Estate at Cranborne (the gardens of this elegant Georgian house featured in the BBC Television series, Hidden Gardens), is convinced that Pelting's classic connections have played a significant part in her enormous success in the paddocks.

Pelting and her descendants have bred the winners of well over fifty Group races worldwide. So far six of them have won at Group 1 level in five countries, the first being West Blagdon-bred Bassenthwaite (Middle Park Stakes). He has been followed by Braashee (French St. Leger), Central Park (Italian Derby), Keen Hunter (Prix de l'Abbaye de Longchamp), Moon Ballad (Dubai World Cup), and Rebelline (Tattersalls' Gold Cup).

The Wigans have always specialised in selling foals at Tattersalls' December Sales and they have sold more than seventy of Pelting's descendants for over 5m guineas. It is a remarkably prolific family and invariably any major domestic sales' catalogue includes some of her descendants, with any females selling for a premium – any self respecting breeder would covet a broodmare of this ilk.

Pelting's trainer, Arthur Budgett, and jockey, Stan Clayton, have a unique link. The former, who followed Dick Dawson (trainer of Mumtaz Mahal) at Whatcombe and preceded Paul Cole (trainer of Ruby Tiger) there, bred and trained the half-brothers, Blakeney and Morston – and Windmill Girl, the dam of these two Derby winners, was bred by Lionel Holliday for whom Stan Clayton was stable jockey.

PETITE ETOILE

Grey, 1956, by Petition - Star of Iran

Owners: Prince Aly Khan, H.H. Aga Khan IV
Trainer: Sir Noel Murless
Jockeys: Lester Piggott, Doug Smith
Breeders: H.H. Aga Khan III, Prince Aly Khan

It seems incongruous that a filly who was beaten eight lengths on her two-year-old début in a match at Manchester's now defunct Castle Irwell racecourse one cold, wet afternoon in May, would be regarded by Prince Aly Khan (joint owner with his son, Karim), as faster than his father's celebrated grey, Mumtaz Mahal, who just happened to be her fourth dam.

A couple of successes at Sandown Park over the minimum distance as a juvenile gave absolutely no indication that Petite Etoile was a filly with classic potential. But with Lester Piggott forsaking the grey to ride her better fancied stable-companion, Collyria, in the One Thousand Guineas, she prevailed at Newmarket partnered by Doug Smith to score by a length from the favourite, Rosalba, with the Aly Khan's first string, Paraguana, in third place.

Although there were grave misgivings that a filly in-bred to Lady Josephine could stay the Oaks' distance, Piggott switched from Collyria to Petite Etoile at Epsom, where the 'little star' came home three lengths clear of the favourite, Cantelo, who was destined to win the St. Leger. It was the beginning of one of the most glamorous partnerships of the 20th century.

Unbeaten in her six outings that season, culminating with the Sussex Stakes, Yorkshire Oaks and Champion Stakes, Petite Etoile proceeded to win the Coronation Cup in each of the next two seasons - the first of these two encounters at Epsom was an historic one as Petite Etoile simply toyed with the previous year's Derby winner, Parthia, to win in the proverbial canter.

It was also a poignant occasion as Aly Khan had been killed in a motoring accident in the Paris suburbs on the night of Thursday, May 12, three weeks earlier. At the time the grey filly was just one of four animals that he and his son had with Noel Murless, and she only remained in training for another season as the big string of homebred horses in France with Alec Head was proving rather disappointing following an unprecedented run of success.

These Coronation Cup victories gave the impression that Petite Etoile, who owed the first part of her name to her sire, Petition, and the second to the name of her dam, Star of Iran, stayed one-and-a-half miles, but the truth was she never really got that distance in a truly run race; with a great turn of foot, she was undoubtedly at her most effective over 10 furlongs. A prima donna, she liked to come late, but appeared to find little off the bridle.

Never out of the first two in nineteen starts, her most memorable reversal came in the King George VI and Queen Elizabeth Stakes as a four-year-old when at 5-2 on she was beaten half a length by the five-year-old entire, Aggressor, on unsuitably soft ground. The general consensus was that Lester Piggott had ridden an injudicious race and given the filly too much to do. Asked his opinion on unsaddling, his laconic reply was, "I think they cut the grass the wrong way." But in the weighing-room the word was that, just for once, Lester had been 'carved up' by his colleagues.

That proved to be her third and final outing of the season as she missed her subsequent engagements due to the coughing epidemic that autumn. Her enforced absence from the Queen Elizabeth II Stakes, run that year at Newbury due to the building of a new grandstand at Ascot (which has just been demolished!), enabled another grey, Sovereign Path, to gain the biggest success of his career.

Petite Etoile's undoubted brilliance was tempered with a

highly strung and wilful disposition as Noel Murless related in his biography. "She was a peculiar animal. She was grey and she loved to have a grey in front of her in the string and, more particularly, a grey behind her when she went out to exercise. In my experience this was unique, but then Petite Etoile was unique in every way.

"How Aly loved that filly and how she loved him too, but my word, how she hated strangers. I remember Cyril Hall, who was Aly's stud manager in those days, coming into Warren Place one December Sales and walking into her box. He said, 'You're getting a bit fat old girl!' He pushed his finger into her neck and she turned round like lightning and got hold of the lapels of his coat and lifted him off the ground. Frightened the life out of him!"

Like her great-great-grandam, Mumtaz Mahal, Petite Etoile invariably had a gelding as a travelling companion as outings to the races proved traumatic right from the start. Noel Murless recalled the filly's début at Manchester. "She got loose twice on the way up from the stables to the course and then she got loose again in the paddock. I am not sure whether she didn't get loose again at the start!"

Petite Etoile's fifteen-year stud innings proved as disastrous as her racing career was brilliant with just one solitary winner to her credit. But perseverance reaped its own reward and, at the age of eighteen, she produced her last foal, the grey Habitat filly, Zahra. One of her dam's only two runners (from three offspring to attain racing age), she became the grandam of Karim Aga Khan's homebred, Zainta, winner of the 1998 Prix de Diane (French Oaks), and Prix Saint-Alary.

Noel Murless' daughter, Julie Cecil, remembers Petite Etoile with great affection. "She arrived at Warren Place as a yearling because Prince Aly was a pal of Dad's and wanted him to have a couple of yearlings. Luckily no one in France wanted her and she came with another filly called Rose Pale. From the age of three onwards she was cared for by Johnny Morgan, a cousin of the singer, Tom Jones. She was a great character and never forgot her friends."

PETONG

Grey, 1980, by Mansingh - Iridium

Owner: Tom Warner
Trainer: Michael Jarvis
Jockey: Bruce Raymond
Breeder: Red House Stud

It was fortuitous that when Britain's leading sire of two-year-olds, Mummy's Pet, died at Barleythorpe Stud, Oakham, Rutland, in the autumn of 1986, there was a ready made replacement in the wings with the grey Petong – he had retired to stand alongside Mummy's Pet only the previous year.

For two decades Barleythorpe Stud was one of the leading commercial stallion studs in the country. Owned by David Gibson, one time president and chairman of the Thoroughbred Breeders' Association and a member of a well known family of equine veterinary surgeons, he had two joint partners in Robert Percival of Glen Andred Stud in Northamptonshire, and Tom Warner of Red House Stud, at Exning, outside Newmarket.

Not only was Tom Warner the breeder of Petong, but he also stood his sire, Mansingh (a former Barleythorpe stallion), at his Red House Stud. In fact he sold the grey in his annual yearling consignment at the 1981 Doncaster St. Leger Sales for 15,000 guineas, but agreed to take him back when some dissatisfaction was expressed by Con Collins, the Irish trainer who had purchased him.

Not a precocious two-year-old himself when his inadequacies were attributed to a particularly virulent bout of the virus, Petong brought off the elusive Wokingham Stakes Stewards' Cup double as a four-year-old, but it was his final, short head, victory in that season's Haydock Park Sprint Cup (then Group 2), from two spectacular sprinters, Habibti and Never So Bold, that warranted his retirement to Barleythorpe.

David Gibson described him as follows, "He's a very correct horse and a very honest one into the bargain. Actually he is quite sensitive and you can easily upset him. He is certainly not a horse you would ever shout at or bully. In fact, you would never want to scold him as he's always trying to please. In the covering yard you can control him just by looking at him, he's very intelligent."

Like Mansingh, Petong spent his retirement at Red House Stud, by which time a number of his sons had also made their mark at stud. The most successful proved to be Petardia (Champagne Stakes, Coventry Stakes), who was bred by David Gibson and Robert Percival in partnership – he is a great great grandson of Abelia, the very first grey to feature in *Grey Magic*.

Jack Berry trained two grey sons of Petong in the entire Paris House, who just failed to provide the Cockerham trainer with that elusive Group 1 victory before going to stud, and the gelded Palacegate Touch. By the time the latter retired to the Northern Racing College aged thirteen, he had won thirty-three races, just one short of the post-war flat record in Great Britain.

Neither Barleythorpe nor Red House are public (stallion) studs any more. Indeed, Barleythorpe is no longer a stud. It was here that two eccentric gentlemen, the 'Yellow Earl' Lord Lonsdale (instigator of boxing's Lonsdale Belt), and Lord Wavertree, a disciple of astrology, intended to establish the first National Stud, but the plan never came to fruition.

In 2005 Red House Stud had a spectacular Group 1 breeding double with the own-brother, Pastoral Pursuits (July Cup), who had a predetermined stallion career at the National Stud, and Goodricke (Haydock Park Sprint Cup).

PORTLAW

Grey, 1928, by Beresford - Portree

Owner: Sir Abe Bailey
Trainer: Atty Persse
Jockey: Harry Beasley
Breeder: Knockany Stud

A leading owner-breeder in the first half of the 20th century, who never allowed the amputation of both legs in later life to curtail his enjoyment of racing, Sir Abe Bailey is best remembered for those great stayers, Son-in-Law, a dual champion sire, his son Foxlaw and the latter's son, Tiberius.

All three horses stood under the management of Reg Day at Terrace House Stud at the top of Newmarket High Street, now the headquarters of Tattersalls adjacent to Park Paddocks. When their owner died in August 1940, Tiberius and another of his owner's stallions, twelve-year-old Portlaw, were sold at the December Sales, when the latter realised only 1,500 guineas.

The grey was knocked down to Alec Marsh (well known in racing circles as the Jockey Club's senior starter), whose wife, Elisabeth, was to manage the horse for the rest of his days at Clifford Nicholson's Limestone Stud in Lincolnshire. Coincidentally Abe Bailey hailed from South Africa, where he was a prominent figure in political circles (he had participated in the Jameson Raid of 1895), and Clifford Nicholson had extensive farming interests there.

Doubtless encouraged by the fact that the colt owed his grey coat to The Tetrarch, Atty Persse had procured Portlaw, named after a picturesque small town in Co. Waterford, for 1,550 guineas at the Doncaster September Yearling Sales from his breeder, David Roche Browning of Knockany Stud (where his sire, Beresford, stood), nephew of the well known Irish breeders, Stamer and John Gubbins.

The Gubbins family owned two studs in Co. Limerick, Knockany (subsequently spelt Knockaney), and Bruree, where they bred the Derby winning half-brothers, Galtee More and Ard Patrick, and two Grand National winners, Seaman and Come Away. The latter was ridden by Harry Beasley Snr, father of Portlaw's regular partner, also Harry. The latter won the Two Thousand Guineas on Mr. Jinks, and his son, Bobby, won the Grand National on Nicolaus Silver, both greys.

Portlaw, who ran initially unnamed, concluded his two-year-old campaign by winning the Champagne Stakes and the Middle Park Stakes, to earn joint top-weight of 9st 7lbs with Jacopo on the Free Handicap. But two major wins over 6 furlongs were not indicative in this instance of any classic aspirations.

An unplaced favourite in the Two Thousand Guineas, the grey was promptly withdrawn from the Derby. Third over a mile at Royal Ascot in the St. James's Palace Stakes, he then concentrated on sprinting, winning the Nunthorpe Stakes and Challenge Stakes in a match with Diolite – he also finished third in that race as a four-year-old.

Although Portlaw failed to establish a male line, he did become an influential sire of broodmares. Two of the most notable were foaled in 1946, the year of his death – Agin The Law became the dam of Sing Sing, sire of Song and Mummy's Pet; and Malapert produced Pall Mall, sire of Reform, but none were grey.

PRECIPICE WOOD

Grey, 1966, by Lauso - Grecian Garden

Owner: Bobby McAlpine
Trainer: Rosemary Lomax
Jockey: Jimmy Lindley
Breeder: Joan Scott

During the 1960s Joan Scott of Buttermilk Stud, near Barford St. Michael, a part of north Oxfordshire noted for its villages of local Hornton ironstone, became quite a celebrity in the breeding world.

During that period she was responsible for three outstanding horses in the German Derby winner, Luciano; Park Top, a memorable racemare for the late Duke of Devonshire; and Precipice Wood. The latter enabled Rosemary Lomax, a noted point-to-point rider in her day, to become the first lady to train a Royal Ascot winner when scoring in the 1969 King George V Handicap. The former trainer still lives in Baydon, above Lambourn, and the stables where she trained the grey are now the Downs' Equestrian Centre.

The following season Precipice Wood, owned by Bobby McAlpine, a member of the McAlpine engineering clan and named after the best pheasant stand on his Llanarmon Estate in north Wales, returned to the Royal Meeting to annex the Gold Cup from the previous year's Derby winner, Blakeney, the first winner of the Blue Riband to turn out in the Gold Cup for a quarter of a century.

Rosie Lomax recalls, "Precipice Wood was a very nervous

horse and had to be treated tenderly – we never plaited him before racing for this reason. During the winter of his two/three-year-old days, our stable National Hunt jockey, Peter Pickford, used to take him for long hacks all round Russley Park; he would then turn him out in a paddock adjoining the yard. One day he jumped a large five-bar gate to get back to his stable!"

Precipice Wood, who was sold from Buttermilk as a foal for 1,200 guineas and resold as a yearling for 2,800 guineas, was out of Grecian Garden, whose dam, Academia, was one of Buttermilk's two foundation mares. A grey, she had been procured privately and unseen for just £400 during the war through Pat Honner – he used to live at Lovelocks, a house now hidden from view at Junction 14 of the M4.

Grecian Garden, who lived to the ripe old age of twenty-nine, also bred Champion Hurdle runner-up, Spartan General, and he and Precipice Wood both became influential jumping sires. Bobby McAlpine also acquired Precipice Wood's own-brother, Coed Cochion (Welsh for Precipice Wood) and this grey provided him with another Royal Ascot victory in the Queen Alexandra Stakes, Britain's longest flat race.

Precipice Wood stood in England, Ireland and Wales in turn. It was at Emral Stud, near Wrexham, that he had a fatal heart attack at the relatively early age of fourteen. Having just covered a full complement of mares, he had been receiving treatment for a stomach complaint. He is best remembered as the sire of Forgive 'N Forget, hero of the 1985 Cheltenham Gold Cup (sold by Bobby McAlpine in utero); he is also the maternal grandsire of the 2001 Grand National winner, Red Marauder.

Few breeders, large or small, have made the sort of contribution that Joan Scott managed at the Thoroughbred Breeders' Association's annual awards. In 1973 Precipice Wood won the two awards for British-based jumping sires, while his dam, Grecian Garden, won the National Hunt Broodmare of the Year award.

PROCLAMATION

Grey, 2002, by King's Best - Shamarra

Owners: Princess Haya of Jordan, Abdullah Saeed Belhab
Trainer: Jeremy Noseda
Jockey: Mick Kinane
Breeder: Cathal M. Ryan

M ost seasons spawn another fine specimen of a grey and 2005 was the turn of Proclamation. Once considered a Derby candidate, this progressive three-year-old staked his claim as one of the country's leading milers in winning the prestigious Sussex Stakes at the Goodwood festival meeting in July.

Not a vintage 'Glorious Goodwood' so far as the weather was concerned, Proclamations dark grey coat hardly made him conspicuous in the mist and gloom, but his devastating run from last to first down the rain sodden straight was evident enough as he denied the gallant mare, Soviet Song, a second successive Sussex Stakes victory.

This was a memorable occasion for all the colt's connections, not least Sheikh Mohammed, who had been experiencing a comparatively lean spell with his Godolphin runners. Previously the grey had won three of his only four outings for an associate, but Goodwood was the first occasion that he had carried the green colours of the sheikh's wife, a delighted Princess Haya of Jordan, daughter of the late King Hussein.

It also provided a needle match between two leading Irish jockeys as Mick Kinane got first run on Soviet Song's partner, Johnny Murtagh – he had ridden Proclamation on his previous start when winning the Jersey Stakes staged at York due to Ascot's rebuilding programme. This was a fourth Sussex Stakes success in eight years for Kinane, following Among Men, Giants Causeway and Rock of Gibraltar.

Godolphin themselves had won the Sussex Stakes with the grey Aljabr and another winner during the nineties was First Island. The latter had been a yearling purchase by John Ferguson for Mollers Racing and he had secured Proclamation on behalf of the Maktoum tribe for 84,000 guineas at the Newmarket October Yearling Sales.

Only the previous week Jeremy Noseda, himself a former member of the Godolphin operation, had saddled Carry On Katie to win the Cheveley Park Stakes for Sheikh Mohammed's son, Mohammed Rashid. There is a further connection between the two horses as both were bred by Cathal Ryan at his Swordlestown Stud, Naas, Co. Kildare.

Proclamation belongs to one of the original Aga Khan families going back at seven generations to Teresina. Like the great grey filly, Mumtaz Mahal, she was acquired as a yearling back in the 1920s from Lady Sykes of Sledmere. The outstanding Aga Khan-bred from this tap-root in recent times is Sendawar.

Immediately after Proclamation's Sussex Stakes victory, Jeremy Noseda, commented, "I'm delighted to win a Group 1 and thrilled to bring this horse through. We had big hopes for him for a long time and to finally deliver him here at this point is a huge thrill. I hope he could run in the Queen Elizabeth II Stakes and the Breeders Cup Mile, but Ill have to talk to Sheikh Mohammed."

QUORUM

Grey, 1954, by Vilmorin - Akimbo

Owner: Thomas Farr
Trainer: Wilfred Lyde
Jockey: Alec Russell
Breeder: Thomas Farr

Quorum was put down at Littleton Stud in Hampshire in 1971 suffering from laminitis. Two years later, his son, Red Rum, gained the first of his three Grand National victories, which, together with two seconds in the world's most famous steeplechase, made him the greatest ever exponent over Aintree's formidable fences.

Littleton Stud, just north of Winchester, was owned by Bruce Deane, and it was here that his father, Gerald, stood a number of Lord Astor's horses before the war. At different times both were partners in bloodstock auctioneers, Tattersalls, and it was at the 1964 Newmarket December Sales that Bruce had acquired Quorum for 10,500 guineas, the grey stallion having completed his first six covering seasons at Balreask Stud, Co. Meath.

Selling stallions at public auction has always been regarded as a last resort as any horse of consequence in search of a new home is invariably sold privately. However, the circumstances surrounding Quorum were different as he was bought to replace his own sire, Vilmorin, who had died the previous year. He too had gone to Littleton after starting off at stud in Ireland.

Whereas Vilmorin was a sprinter, Quorum was a miler. Runner-up to Crepello in the Two Thousand Guineas, beaten half a length, after winning the Free Handicap, he then won the Sussex Stakes and Jersey Stakes, and at the following year's Royal Meeting he finished third in the Queen Anne Stakes and second in the Rous Memorial Stakes, the opening races on the Tuesday and Friday respectively.

Quorum's regular partner, Alec Russell, who was also associated with another northern trained grey in Warpath, had completed his apprenticeship at Lamorlaye with John Torterolo, the trainer of another *Grey Magic* celebrity in Taj Mah.

By a strange twist of fate, Quorum, who did commendably well at Littleton (now owned by Jeff Smith of Lochsong and Persian Punch renown), died in May 1971 and within two weeks his owner-breeder, Thomas Farr, of Ruddington Grange, Nottingham, was also dead. He and his cousin, Bryan Farr of Worksop Manor Stud, had been co directors of the family's local Home Brewery at Daybrook.

It was from Vilmorin that Quorum inherited his grey colouring as did Thomas Farr's excellent homebred sprinter Vigo, who was a very close relative. Whereas the majority of Vigo's progeny took after their sire, Quorum's offspring won over all sorts of distances and he had an exceptional grey juvenile in the unbeaten Quarryknowe, but all his many winners are totally overshadowed by Red Rum.

Unbelievably Red Rum had dead-heated at Liverpool when successful on his two-year-old début over five furlongs, the day before the debacle of Foinavon's Grand National. He was then trained by Tim Molony for Maurice Kingsley in whose colours Tim had won three Champion Hurdles on Sir Ken. Ironically Red Rum's next owner, Lurline Brotherton, had owned the 1950 'National winner, Freebooter, regarded at that time as the quintessential Aintree 'chaser.

RAFFINGORA

Grey, 1965, by Grey Sovereign - Cameo

Owner: Monty Stevens
Trainer: Bill Marshall
Jockey: Lester Piggott
Breeder: Eveton Stud

A World War II fighter pilot with a DFC, Bill Marshall is the only trainer to have sent out winners from four continents, Europe, Australia, Africa and the Americas – he is now based in Barbados.

Bill did particularly well with 'second hand' horses purchased at the Newmarket Autumn horses-in-training sale and two greys with whom he excelled for Monty Stevens, a Wiltshire dairy farmer and noted Friesian breeder, were My Swanee and the amazing Raffingora. Another grey purchased in training at Ascot Sales was Grey Mirage, the sire of Desert Orchid.

Raffingora was a useful juvenile who had scored at the Epsom Derby Meeting and at Goodwood for Geoffrey Brooke, brother-in-law of The Tetrarch's trainer, Atty Persse, but having won only once the ensuing season for Brooke's successor, Doug Smith, he was sold by his breeder, Anthony Samuel, for only 1,800 guineas.

Transferred to Bill Marshall, then based at Ogbourne Maisey, north of Marlborough, where Peter Makin now trains, Raffingora was to prove a sensational sprinter and Timeform's annual publication *Racehorses* has seldom been more effusive in singing a horse's praises.

'Raffingora's brilliant achievements over the past two seasons earned him a place among the immortals of the Turf. His tremendous record in that time – seventeen wins from twenty-eight starts – is all the more impressive when one considers that the majority of his races were handicaps in which he nearly always had 10st or more to carry. To the amazement of almost everyone, he kept on winning in the face of stiffer and stiffer treatment from the handicappers.

'In 1970 Raffingora's achievements were remarkable. He won more races than any other horse in training and put up the most spectacular handicap performance of the season when winning the Cherkley Sprint at Epsom, where he recorded the fastest five furlongs ever electrically timed (53.89 secs). He also won two of the most important weight-for-age sprints of the season, the Temple Stakes at Sandown and the King George Stakes at Goodwood. It is not hard to see why he ranks as one of the most popular horses ever to race in this country.'

As a syndicated stallion, Raffingora retired to stand at his owner's Lucknam Park Stud, between Bath and Chippenham, where Monty Stevens took out a licence to train himself. Known as the invisible trainer as he never went racing, his runners were invariably saddled by his son, Jeffrey, and one of the most prolific winners was Raffingora's son, Vilgora.

Nowadays, Lucknam Park is a luxury country house hotel, but at one time it was owned by Graham Beck, the South African whose bloodstock interests also embraced the famous Gainesway Farm in Kentucky.

Raffingora was exported to Japan in 1973 before his first crop of runners ever appeared on the racecourse. He sired a top two-year-old from each of his first two crops with the colt, Overtown, and the filly, Pasty, and another son, Raffindale, excelled in Australia – all greys. Overtown was named after the stud at Wroughton, near Swindon, where Raffingora was bred by Tony Samuel trading as Eveton Stud.

RIGHT BOY

Grey, 1954, by Impeccable - Happy Ogan

Owners: Geoffrey Gilbert, Sir David Wills
Trainers: Bill Dutton, Pat Rohan
Jockey: Lester Piggott
Breeder: William J. Byrne

Unbelievable as it may seem, Grove Cottage Stables, in the North Yorkshire training centre of Malton, provided the winner of the July Cup, the mid-summer jewel in the sprinting crown, in five of the six years from 1955 to 1960, with Pappa Fourway, Vigo, Right Boy and Tin Whistle. Both Vigo and dual scorer, Right Boy, were greys.

The champion sprinter of 1958 and 1959, following four consecutive wins as a juvenile, Right Boy had gained his first prestige victory in the King's Stand Stakes at Royal Ascot, but thereafter his three-year-old career was disrupted by a poisoned leg. However, the following season he gained six successive wins, the first and last of them at Birmingham, the home of his bookmaker owner, Geoffrey Gilbert.

In the interim he won the Cork and Orrery Stakes, July Cup, King George Stakes and Nunthorpe Stakes, all races which now carry Group status. That December, Bill Dutton died unexpectedly, whereupon the stable was taken over by his future son-in-law, Pat Rohan, who saddled Right Boy to win these four sprint classics on successive outings as a five-year-old.

At Goodwood and York, the grey carried the colours of David Wills, the owner of Hadrian Stud, Newmarket (now owned by Sheikh Mohammed), and a member of the Bristol tobacco family, having procured him for a reputed £30,000 through the British Bloodstock Agency. This was a handsome return on the 575 guineas that the colt had originally cost as a yearling in Ireland when secured from his breeder by local agent, Bertie Kerr.

Right Boy, who was ridden to all bar one of his sixteen victories by Lester Piggott, stood first at Sandwich Stud, Newmarket (now an extension of Cheveley Park Stud), and then at Limestone Stud in Lincolnshire – he was put down aged twenty-three in 1977. Like many unfashionably bred horses, he was not a successful sire, but three of his progeny to win at Goodwood were Right Strath (King George Stakes), Village Boy (Richmond Stakes), and Reet Lass (Molecomb Stakes).

One of the first mares that Right Boy ever covered was another grey, Scargill, whose owner, a fruit and vegetable merchant from Smethwick, where Geoff Gilbert was born, bet the Birmingham bookmaker that the resultant foal would not be grey. Sure enough he collected when the mare produced a chesnut filly, but within six months she had turned to grey!

Geoff Gilbert, who died aged eighty-one in 2004, was one of the great characters of the bookmaking fraternity and the family business is still thriving. A teenager when starting to run an illegal book on the streets, he appeared before the magistrates on his 17th birthday to be given a £10 fine!

Right Boy's other owner, David Wills, started off on a high note with the One Thousand Guineas winner, Happy Laughter. She proved a bitter disappointment as a broodmare, but he had the rare distinction of breeding a Kentucky Derby winner in Tomy Lee. His bloodstock interests have been continued by his daughter, Dr. Catherine Wills, trading as St. Clare Hall Stud.

ROAN ROCKET

Grey, 1961, by Buisson Ardent - Farandole II

Owner: Tommy Frost
Trainer: George Todd
Jockey: Lester Piggott
Breeder: Lady Ainsworth

In March 1962 Sir Thomas Ainsworth of Ballinakill, Adare, Co. Limerick, won the Champion Hurdle with the grey Anzio; that October his wife, May, sold a grey yearling colt (then described as chesnut or roan) by Buisson Ardent out of Farandole II at Tattersalls' October Sales for 1,800 guineas.

The first of four lots consigned by his breeder, Roan Rocket was already named when he was knocked down to Tommy Frost, who worked in the Lloyds' insurance market in the City, and the colt joined Manton maestro, George Todd, whose considerable reputation as a trainer was established largely with durable old stayers, amongst them the popular Trelawny.

Roan Rocket, however, was a miler and an exact contemporary of another colt who excelled over that distance in Derring-Do. Never entered for the classics, Roan Rocket still won two major prizes in the summer of his three-year-old career, the St James's Palace Stakes and Sussex Stakes – Derring-Do was runner-up at Goodwood. A rheumatic problem restricted him to only three outings that season.

Back in top form at four years, Roan Rocket won the Hungerford Stakes and was second in the Eclipse Stakes, beaten a short head by Canisbay, and in the Sussex Stakes; he also dead-heated with Derring-Do for third place in the Lockinge Stakes. Equipped with blinkers on his finale, he was unplaced behind Derring-Do in the Queen Elizabeth II Stakes having been decidedly mulish at the start.

Following a solitary season at Derisley Wood Stud, the grey was then transferred to neighbouring Dunchurch Lodge Stud as a replacement for the homebred St. Leger hero, Premonition. The former had been in retirement there for three years when he died in 1986 aged twenty-five.

In January 1993 Dunchurch Lodge became the last piece of Sir Alec Black's old Compton Park Stud, which had also comprised Dalham Hall, Hadrian, Derisley Wood and Someries, to be acquired by Sheikh Mohammed, whereupon it reverted to its original name, Rockingham.

Tommy Frost retained 60 per cent of Roan Rocket when he retired to stud with the remainder owned by Michael Wyatt's Dunchurch Lodge Stud Company – in 1972 they sponsored the Roan Rocket Plate for two-year-olds on the July Course at Newmarket with all the entrance money being donated to the Equine Research Station at Balaton Lodge.

Roan Rocket made his mark at stud and his grey son, Gairloch, continued the good work standing in France. Two Dunchurch Lodge-bred daughters to do well were Catherine Wheel and Negligence. The former won the Nassau Stakes and Musidora Stakes, while the latter became the dam of Negligent, a grey who finished third in the 1990 One Thousand Guineas. Another grey filly, Rory's Rocket, won the Queen Mary Stakes.

ROOSTER BOOSTER

Grey, 1994, by Riverwise - Came Cottage

Owner: Terry Warner
Trainer: Philip Hobbs
Jockey: Richard Johnson
Breeder: Elsie Mitchell

It must be galling for any small trainer to see two former stable stars go on to Cheltenham to win the Gold Cup and the Champion Hurdle, but that is precisely what happened to Richard Mitchell with Cool Ground in 1992 and Rooster Booster in 2003 respectively.

Rooster Booster was particularly special as not only did Richard's wife, Elsie, breed him, but they also stood his sire, Riverwise, at their home in the Dorset village of Piddletrenthide, near Dorchester, and he had been ridden to his very first victory at Taunton by their daughter, Sophie, a very competent professional jockey, now retired.

Only the third grey since the war to win the Champion Hurdle following Anzio in 1962 and Kribensis in 1990, and the eldest at nine years of age, Rooster Booster had been sold privately by the Mitchells for £60,000 to Terry Warner. The patron of Philip Hobbs' Somerset stable had originally offered £50,000, but agreed the asking price subject to a satisfactory veterinary examination that was not as thorough as it might have been due to the grey's aversion to members of that profession!

The only notable produce by the Riverman horse, Riverwise, whom the Mitchells acquired cheaply as a four-year-old at the

Doncaster Sales in 1992 (he never ran on the flat due to a stalls' phobia), Rooster Booster had won the County Hurdle at the preceding Cheltenham festival, and prefaced his Champion Hurdle victory by eleven lengths with successes in the Bula and Agfa Hurdles.

Also second twice in the Grade 1 Aintree Hurdle, the grey progressed to the top of the tree through handicaps, and three times he finished runner-up in the Tote Gold Trophy. In 2004 he suffered an agonising short head defeat at Newbury under top-weight in what is always one of the most competitive affairs of the entire season.

Rooster Booster's dam, Came Cottage, made her mark in another sphere, winning four point-to-points, ridden by one or other of the Mitchells' two sons, Nicholas and Timothy. Their father had originally bought Came Cottage from her breeder, Nigel Martin (one of his owners), after she had broken down – subsequently she fractured a hind fetlock and spent eleven months confined to her box.

The fact that Rooster Booster has been restricted to hurdles surprised his original handler, Richard Mitchell, as initially, being a good jumper, it had been the intention to run him between the flags. But the gelding had his idiosyncrasies. "When he was a youngster he was an absolute comedian," said Richard. "The first time he did a proper bit of work, he shot out from behind two lead horses, chased one of my owners round a tree, and then caught the horses up on the gallop."

The handsome grey enabled the Mitchell family to take away two coveted trophies at the Thoroughbred Breeders' Association's annual awards' dinner in London for the 2002/03 season. As the season's leading NH sire and broodmare respectively, Riverwise won the Whitbread Silver Salver and Came Cottage won the Dudgeon Cup.

In 2004 Rooster Booster was a beaten favourite when second in the Champion Hurdle, thus failing to emulate Hatton's Grace and Sea Pigeon, both of whom won the Champion Hurdle as

10-year-olds. The following year he never looked likely to become only the second hurdler after Comedy of Errors to regain his crown. The Irish invader, Hardy Eustace, scored on both occasions.

Latterly Rooster Booster never seemed to have races run to suit him – ideally he liked to come late off a strong pace, but he remained a great favourite with the public. Indeed he was held in such high esteem that the Cheltenham executive named a special all-in deal for racegoers in his honour, The Rooster Booster Raceday Admission Package.

The 'will he, won't he be retired' scenario persisted after Rooster Booster had finally got back on the winning trail at Sandown Park on the eve of the 2005 Betfred Gold Cup. It was then decided to let him take his chance the following week in the former Swinton Hurdle at Haydock Park, the first big event of the new season – and fourth place seemed to put pending retirement off the agenda altogether.

ROYAL MINSTREL

Grey, 1925, by Tetratema - Harpsichord

Owners: George P. Gough, John Hay Whitney
Trainer: Sir Cecil Boyd-Rochfort
Jockey: Joe Childs
Breeder: James Maher

Considering that Cecil Boyd-Rochfort was subsequently appointed the Royal trainer and was knighted for his services to racing, it was something of a coincidence that the first good horse he trained at his Freemason Lodge stables, Newmarlet (now occupied by another knight, Michael Stoute), should be called Royal Minstrel.

The Captain, as he was always known (he had served briefly in the Scots Guards), always regarded Royal Minstrel, a big, rather heavy shouldered individual, as the best he ever handled up to one-and-a-quarter miles and he was owned initially by a distant relation of his mother's, George Gough.

Playing the tables at the casino in Monte Carlo one evening, George Gough had the exceeding good fortune to win £10,000, whereupon he immediately instructed cousin, Cecil, to buy him a yearling up to this amount – a sum he lost at a later gambling session. Although he had only wanted to acquire one yearling, Cecil prevailed upon him to purchase two for the same outlay.

In 1926 in the old Glasgow Paddocks, Doncaster, Boyd-Rochfort acquired a brace of colts from Jim Maher's draft of five – the Newmarket trainer always had a high regard for the stock bred by his fellow Irishman, who was very much in the news as the breeder and consignor of the previous year's Derby winner, Manna.

The first of his two purchases, a son of Phalaris costing 5,200 guineas, proved of no consequence, but the second at 4,200 guineas was Royal Minstrel. As a youngster the son of Tetratema was very highly strung with a disarming habit of rearing and generally misbehaving on the Heath. But with perseverance and the opportunity to have a pick of grass before working on the gallops, his attitude changed for the better.

An easy winner of the Craven Stakes on his début, he was only beaten a head in the Two Thousand Guineas by Flamingo. Unplaced in the Derby, he then won the St James's Palace Stakes back at a mile. First time out the following year, he won the Victoria Cup at Hurst Park (now a Thames-side housing estate), whereupon George Gough sold him to one of the stable's leading American patrons, John Hay Whitney.

The grey then won the Cork and Orrery Stakes and Eclipse Stakes, trouncing the great Fairway by four lengths on the latter occasion – in between he was just beaten by the diminutive filly, Tiffin, in a memorable renewal for the July Cup. Finally he succumbed narrowly to the grey, Tag End, when runner-up in the Nunthorpe Stakes. His regular partner, Joe Childs, features in *Grey Magic* as the racing owner of the distinguished foundation mare, Jojo.

Royal Minstrel remained Jock Whitney's property for the remainder of his life. Like the colt's breeder, Jim Maher, this popular Anglophile, who was the American Ambassador to Britain, did well with jumpers before turning to the flat and between the wars he owned two outstanding 'chasers in Easter Hero and Thomond II.

Initially Royal Minstrel stood in the USA, but in 1936 his American-bred daughter, Night Song, homebred by Jock Whitney at his Greentree Stud in Kentucky, won the Queen Mary Stakes. Another grey, she used to spend much of her time fly-jumping out at exercise and that autumn such high spirits caused her undoing. One day she got loose on the Heath, galloped riderless back towards Freemason Lodge and was killed crossing the Bury Road.

Night Song's sire was then repatriated to stand in Newmarket at Heath Lodge Stud for the 1939 season, but died in August of the following year. Coincidentally he provides the all-important link to Indian Skimmer's grey inheritance and she was trained by Boyd-Rochfort's stepson, Henry Cecil.

RUBY TIGER

Grey, 1987, by Ahonoora - Hayati

Owner: Susan Blacker
Trainer: Paul Cole
Jockey: Richard Quinn
Breeders: Steven Stanhope, Sheikh M. Alamuddin

Susan Blacker's much travelled grey Ruby Tiger was making her third appearance in Tattersalls' Park Paddocks when the second top-priced filly at 220,000 guineas at the 1993 Newmarket December Sales en route to a stud career in Japan – the highest priced filly at 270,000 guineas was another grey, Nicer.

Six years earlier the daughter of Ahonoora had been sold for 33,000 guineas at the corresponding sale as a foal from Dooneen Stud, Co. Limerick, owned by Steven Stanhope. His father, Lord Harrington of neighbouring Greenmount Stud, used to buy yearlings for Sir David Robinson of Radio Rentals, who at one time was the biggest owner in England with three private trainers at Newmarket.

Ruby Tiger was originally bought by Philip Blacker and his wife to sell on as a yearling and before being resubmitted at the Highflyer (better known as the Houghton) Sales, the filly spent the intervening period with Susan's father, Colin Davies, at his Oakgrove stables, near Chepstow. Now a stud owned by John Deer, the owner-breeder of Averti and Patavellian, this is where Colin Davies trained triple champion hurdler, Persian War.

The son of Sir Cecil 'Monkey' Blacker, who was a proficient amateur rider, both on the racecourse and in the show ring,

Philip Blacker first made his name as a professional jump jockey (his name is synonymous with that good staying 'chaser, Royal Mail), who retired to become an even more distinguished sculptor – his handiwork includes the statues of Desert Orchid at Kempton Park and Red Rum at Aintree.

When Ruby Tiger failed to match her foal price as a yearling, the Blackers bought out Colin Davies, who then owned a ²/₃rd share, and sold a 50% interest to their neighbour, Lord Donoughmore, and she duly went into training with Paul Cole at Whatcombe, once home to the illustrious grey filly, Mumtaz Mahal.

"Ruby Tiger provided us with the most incredible fun for the five years she was running," says Philip. "We travelled the world with her. She won or was placed in Group races in England, Ireland, Italy, France, Germany, Canada and the USA, winning nine in all and some £600,000."

Although she never won at Group 1 level, she actually won the Nassau Stakes, which has since been elevated to Group 1 status, in two consecutive years – a third successive attempt in 1993 was thwarted when she was found to be cast in her box, as well as the E.P. Taylor Stakes at Woodbine, which was subsequently reinstated as a Grade 1 event.

"The E.P. Taylor Stakes was a memorable occasion," Philip recalls. "The problem for us was that after buying out our partner and funding the trip to Toronto, we realised that unless she won or was placed, we couldn't afford to get her home. Sue was dispatched to sweet talk the Woodbine executive, who very kindly said that if she was not in the first three they would pay for her return. In the event it was not necessary as she bolted in by five lengths to win the £90,000 event!"

RUNNYMEDE

Grey, 1961, by Petition - Dutch Clover

Owner: Florence Prior
Trainer: Bill Wightman
Jockey: Duncan Keith
Breeder: Florence Prior

It takes an exceptional two-year-old to bustle up the older generation in the Nunthorpe Stakes, the all-aged sprint championship. So when Runnymede finished third, within $1^1/_2$ lengths of two champion sprint fillies, Matatina, and another grey Secret Step, at York in August 1963 with Sammy Davis fourth, he looked to have a very bright future.

Also successful on three occasions as a juvenile at Newbury, in April, June and September, by an aggregate of fifteen lengths, he was faced with stiff tasks in sprint handicaps the ensuing season, but came back to form on his four-year-old début to win the Palace House Stakes at the Newmarket Guineas Meeting. But then fate conspired against him.

Found in a drowsy condition in his box on the morning of his intended participation in the 1965 King George Stakes at Goodwood – his trainer has always maintained that he must have been 'got at' as there was simply no other plausible explanation – he never ran again, as a strained forearm muscle ended his racing career prematurely.

The son of Petition was homebred by Florence Prior, previously owner of Adstock Manor Stud, near Bletchley, in Buckinghamshire (subsequently famous as the home of High

Line), a great authority on breeding and compiler of the *Half-Bred Stud Book*, the forerunner to what is now called *The Non-Thoroughbred Register*, published by Weatherbys.

By the time Runnymede came along Miss Prior boarded a nucleus of broodmares at Benham Stud, near Newbury, run in those days by Leslie Denton, a dairy farmer, who owned a fine staying 'chaser of the 1950s in Hart Royal, and then taken over by his son, Roger. At one time Leslie Denton also owned Rhonehurst, the well known training yard in Upper Lambourn; one of the descendants of his foundation mare, Port Beam, is Further Flight.

It was at Benham that Sir Richard Sutton stood his 1866 Triple Crown winner, Lord Lyon, and to celebrate his Derby victory the bells were rung at Speen church – unfortunately no one asked the vicar but he was soon placated with a donation of £100! Benham is still owned by the Sutton family and at Stockcross, on the opposite side of the A4 from Benham Park, is the Lord Lyon public house.

Originally Florence Prior put Dutch Clover in training herself, but as her trainer thought she had a dubious temperament, she was sold as a yearling at the Newmarket December Sales for 1,300 guineas. Winner of the Lancashire Oaks, she then resurfaced at the sales and, after failing to make her 2,000 guineas reserve, her breeder could not resist the temptation of buying her back privately.

Not only was Runnymede bred, foaled and reared at Benham, but he also spent the duration of his stallion life there where he died aged twenty-five – by then his coat was as white as snow. He made his greatest contribution in the long term through his grey daughter, Canton Silk. For Gerald Leigh of Eydon Hall Farm, she bred Brocade, dam of the Irish classic winners, Barathea (Breeders' Cup Mile) and his own-sister, Gossamer.

SARITAMER

Grey, 1971, by Dancer's Image - Irish Chorus

Owner: Charles St. George
Trainer: Vincent O'Brien
Jockey: Lester Piggott
Breeder: Mrs. Bruce M. Donaldson

Wyld Court, Hampstead Norreys, north of Newbury, where Sir William Cooke bred his 1946 Two Thousand Guineas winner, Happy Knight, has had rather a chequered innings since then. Owned at one time by entrepreneurs, Peter de Savary and Green Shield Stamps creator, Richard Tompkins, it is now the site of the Wyld Court Rainforest, which replicates a tropical rainforest under glass.

During the 1970s it was a thriving public (stallion) stud owned by an anonymous Middle East consortium, standing two Charles St. George flag-bearers, Lorenzaccio and Saritamer. Previously the stud had been owned by Mary Marshall, wife of top jump jockey, Bryan Marshall, and the new set-up was managed by one of the latter's riding colleagues, Dave Dick.

To Lorenzaccio, Wyld Court Stud bred Ahonoora, whose son, Indian Ridge, has become one of the most important stallions in Europe, while Saritamer, despite an absolutely brilliant racing career and all the other more obvious credentials to make a successful stallion, disappeared without trace, but for one very notable exception.

The American-bred grey, who had cost $50,000 as a yearling at Saratoga, was a smart two-year-old winning two Group races at the Curragh, before finishing fourth to another grey, Habat, in the Middle Park Stakes. Next season he proved a brilliant sprinter, but over 6 furlongs rather than five, winning the Cork and Orrery Stakes, July Cup and Diadem Stakes.

Syndicated to stand at Wyld Court, Saritamer had a most attractive pedigree, by Native Dancer's son, Dancer's Image, disqualified 'winner' of the Kentucky Derby, from the immediate family of Noblesse, runaway ten lengths winner of the 1963 Oaks. In 1982 Saritamer was responsible for an Oaks winner of his own in Time Charter, but not long after he was banished to Saudi Arabia following an interim period at Aston Park Stud and Southcourt Stud.

Meanwhile, Time Charter proceeded to win the King George VI and Queen Elizabeth Stakes, Champion Stakes and Coronation Cup – two of her offspring, Zinaad and Time Allowed, have won the Jockey Club Stakes for Time Charter's breeder, Robert Barnett. Based in Germany, Zinaad is the sire of 2002 One Thousand Guineas and Oaks heroine, Kazzia.

Saritamer's retirement to stud more than thirty years ago was the first significant indication of the colossal Arab involvement that was to erupt upon the breeding scene in Britain over the ensuing decades.

This was predicted by *Daily Express* racing journalist and BBC television commentator, Clive Graham. Writing about Saritamer in 1974, he predicted, "The purchase of this potential stallion will trigger off similar deals in the next year or so. The money is there and religious barriers against involvement in gambling activities are gradually being lowered. It is only this single factor which has retarded the whole operation." Prophetic words!

SECRET STEP

Grey, 1959, by Native Dancer - Tap Day

Owner: Paul Mellon
Trainer: Peter Hastings-Bass
Jockeys: Geoff Lewis, Scobie Breasley
Breeder: Paul Mellon

The great Mill Reef was not the first homebred champion that the popular American Anglophile, Paul Mellon, had in training at Park House, Kingsclere, next to Watership Down, in Hampshire, although he is the one that everyone remembers. Watership Down is now almost as famous for the Lloyd-Webbers' stud of that name as for those ubiquitous rabbits!

It was in 2003 that Andrew Balding took over the licence at Kingsclere from his father, Ian Balding, who trained Mill Reef, but it was the latter's father-in-law, Peter Hastings-Bass, a beneficiary of the Bass Brewery fortune, who handled Secret Step - like that great filly, Hula Dancer, she inherited her colour from their sire, Native Dancer.

In 1962 Paul Mellon's striking colours of black, gold cross, front and back (now adopted by the Balding family's Kingsclere Stud where Mellon used to board a handful of broodmares), were carried by Secret Step, who was voted champion sprinter without ever competing in the major sprint races. Originally this handsome individual, who had to be held up for a late run, was regarded as a classic prospect.

That season Secret Step won three consecutive starts culminating with the inaugural Vernons' Gold Cup, then held at the York festival meeting in August before being transferred to

Haydock Park where it has been run under a number of different guises. On that occasion the filly won by a short head with top-weight and had to survive an objection from the runner-up for interference.

As a four-year-old, Secret Step had to share the honours as champion sprinter with another filly, the year junior Matatina. They met on three occasions. On their seasonal reappearance in the King's Stand Stakes, Matatina finished second and Secret Step was fourth. Meeting at weight-for-age, Secret Step then beat the Grey Sovereign filly by three-parts of a length for the July Cup only for the positions to be reversed in the Nunthorpe Stakes - this time the winning margin was a length, with Runnymede, another grey, in third place.

In between Secret Step had won the King George Stakes in brilliant fashion, but it was only after Goodwood that it transpired that her covering by Alcide had proved unsuccessful. In fact she did get in foal to the horse the following year. In 1966 she was then exported to Paul Mellon's Rokeby Farms in Virginia, in foal to Relko, together with a Relko filly foal and little has been heard of them since.

SHADAYID

Grey, 1988, by Shadeed - Desirable

Owner: Sheikh Hamdan Al Maktoum
Trainer: John Dunlop
Jockey: Willie Carson
Breeder: Shadwell Farm Inc.

When Sheikh Hamdan Al Maktoum's Shadayid triumphed in the 1991 One Thousand Guineas at 6-4 on she was the shortest priced favourite since another grey, the French-trained, American-bred, Hula Dancer, scored back in 1963 at 2-1 on.

Undefeated in three juvenile starts culminating with the Prix Marcel Boussac, Shadayid went on to run with the greatest distinction after her Guineas victory, albeit she never won again. Competing exclusively at the highest level, she was second in the Coronation Stakes and Sussex Stakes; third in the Oaks, Queen Elizabeth II Stakes and Haydock Park Sprint Cup.

"She was an exceptionally good two-year-old," her trainer, John Dunlop, relates, "and her three-year-old career was unusual in that she ran at distances between one-and-a-half miles at Epsom and six furlongs at Haydock Park."

Initially, Shadayid was covered at her owner's Shadwell Stud, near Thetford in Norfolk, by the resident stallion, Nashwan, but that was only a fleeting visit as the result of that union, Bint Shadayid, was foaled at Shadwell Farm in Kentucky. So far Bint Shadayid has proved the best of her dam's progeny and she was third in the 1996 One Thousand Guineas.

Vast expenditure on bloodstock can never guarantee success, but it did in the case of Shadayid. It was at the 1986 Keeneland Breeding Stock Sale that Hamdan Al Maktoum paid $1.6m for her dam, Desirable, carrying her second foal, by El Gran Senor. In fact it was anything but an auspicious start as that foal died and so too did the first.

Only two years previously Desirable, who won the Cheveley Park Stakes and was third in the One Thousand Guineas, had been sold to Coolmore as a three-year-old for exactly 1m guineas, which was not only the highest price at that year's Newmarket December Sales, but was also just one bid short of the 1982 record of 1.02m guineas – not a bad return considering the IR10,000 guineas she cost as a yearling.

Desirable was consigned to the sales from Barry Hills' old Lambourn stables at South Bank as the property of a partnership between Catherine Corbett and Robert Sangster – the fact that her half-sister, Park Appeal, had just won the Cheveley Park Stakes certainly helped the price! In 1989, Alydaress, a grey half-sister to Desirable and Park Appeal, won the Irish Oaks.

When Mrs Corbett watched Shadayid winning the One Thousand Guineas did she regret selling the dam? "No, not at all as I would never have sent her to the same stallions," she explained. 'I don't want to breed and I have only stayed in this game by having some jolly good fillies and selling them for a huge profit." And she is quick to give Barry Hills all the credit he deserves.

SHARP EDGE

Grey, 1970, by Silver Shark - Cutle

Owner: Sir John Astor
Trainer: Dick Hern
Jockey: Joe Mercer
Breeder: Sir John Astor

There was a great fanfare of trumpets when it was announced that the British Bloodstock Agency would be standing three newly syndicated stallions at Robert Francis' Sussex Stud for the 1974 covering season with Roi Lear (French Derby), Sharp Edge (Irish Two Thousand Guineas), and Scottish Rifle (Eclipse Stakes).

Part of what was originally the Hornung family's West Grinstead Estate at Horsham, the stud in the interim had served as a stallion annexe for the old National Stud at Gillingham in Dorset. However, its new identity as the Sussex Stud under the management of John Gray, MRCVS, who returned home from Kenya to take up the appointment, was short lived, the three resident stallions soon having to find new homes.

The grey Sharp Edge completed just two covering seasons there before being transferred to Littleton Stud, outside Winchester, where he survived another couple of years before export to Australia – he was originally destined for the National Stud in Spain, but that deal fell through. From his very first crop of foals came Alec Badger's smart grey Shapina – the private sale of her own-sister, Premier Rose, to trainer, Peter Harris, provided sufficient funds for her owner-breeder to buy his previously tenanted Grove Farm, near Witney, in Oxfordshire.

Sharp Edge, who also won the Prix Jean Prat as a three-year-old, when he was third in the Two Thousand Guineas and Champion Stakes, had particular appeal to Australian breeders – some of his relatives, like Hermes and Buoy, were proven stallions in the Antipodes. They are members of the famous Felucca family, developed by Dick Hollingsworth at his now defunct Arches Hall Stud in Hertfordshire.

During Dick's lifetime this family was identified at Arches Hall with staying horses but, since his death in February 2001, it has become much more versatile, other breeders producing the likes of Norse Dancer, a top middle distance performer, and leading juvenile, Mail The Desert – and just for good measure there is also the 2002 Grand National hero, Bindaree.

Dick Hollingsworth and Sir John Astor had been at Eton together, and the latter bred Sharp Edge as a result of an exchange of mares with his old school friend. It proved a very one-sided arrangement. While Dick failed to obtain any benefit, Sharp Edge's dam, Cutle, also bred Jakie his 1981 St. Leger hero, Cut Above.

The half-brothers, Sharp Edge and Cut Above, were both trained by Dick Hern, who was a salaried trainer at West Ilsley in Berkshire, and, at that time, Jakie Astor was his landlord. Nowadays, West Ilsley is owned by international soccer star turned trainer, Mick Channon.

Sharp Edge's jockey, Joe Mercer, has close connections with two *Grey Magic* personalities. At Newbury racecourse in June 1972 he escaped unhurt when the light plane in which he was travelling crashed on take-off killing the pilot, and before the resulting conflagration he rescued the other three passengers, amongst them Raffingora's trainer, Bill Marshall. Harry Carr, rider of two celebrated greys in Grey Sovereign and his son Sovereign Path, was Joe Mercer's father-in-law.

SILKEN GLIDER

Grey, 1954, by Airborne - Silken Slipper

Owner: Joe McGrath
Trainer: Seamus McGrath
Jockey: Jim Eddery
Breeder: McGrath Trust Co.

In 1951 Joe McGrath, one of the dominant personalities of his generation in Irish racing, won the Derby with Arctic Prince, trained at Royston in Hertfordshire by Willie Stephenson, and he came within a short head of winning the 1957 Oaks with the grey Silken Glider, who just failed to beat The Queen's leased filly, Carrozza. Both Arctic Prince and Silken Glider were homebreds.

But there was compensation in store when Silken Glider ran out a convincing winner of the Irish Oaks by four lengths, ridden by Jim Eddery (father of Pat), three weeks later on the Curragh, to become her sire's only really top-class flat winner. Trained at Glencairn Stables, Sandyford, by Seamus McGrath, one of Joe's sons, this is not far from the Curragh where she was bred and raised at the McGrath family's Brownstown Stud.

As a young man, Joe McGrath had fought for Irish independence; he remained a prominent figure in Irish politics as a member of the Dail and in the administration of racing in Ireland as chairman of the Racing Board and a steward of the Turf Club – he was a prime instigator of the Irish Sweeps Derby which helped to make this classic one of the great races in the international racing calendar.

He also enjoyed considerable success as a breeder. It was in 1941 that he bought the Brownstown Stud from Fred Myerscough, a family closely associated with Goffs' bloodstock sales. That same year at the dispersal of Lord Furness' bloodstock, he also spent 14,000 guineas (a colossal sum in those dark years of the war) to secure Carpet Slipper – at the time Joe McGrath also owned her two-year-old, Windsor Slipper; a private yearling acquisition, he was destined to win the Irish Triple Crown.

Windsor Slipper's unraced half-sister, Silken Slipper, is the dam of Silken Glider. There is a certain irony here as Silken Glider's Epsom conqueror, Carrozza, was bred by the National Stud which had previously been Lord Furness' Compton Stud – subsequently it became Simon Wingfield Digby's Sandley Stud and later Prince Fahd Salman's Newgate Stud. The property is now under the auspicies of Alfred Buller of Scarvagh House Stud in Northern Ireland.

Joe McGrath, the man who sold Nasrullah to the USA, died in 1966 and Silken Glider died at Brownstown Stud two years later. Her most noted offspring was the grey Alciglide, whom Seamus McGrath trained to win the Queen Alexandra Stakes and Prix Gladiateur, the two longest flat races in Britain and France respectively. Seamus McGrath died in th summer of 2005.

SILVER PATRIARCH

Grey, 1994, by Saddlers' Hall - Early Rising

Owner: Peter Winfield
Trainer: John Dunlop
Jockey: Pat Eddery
Breeder: Peter Winfield

It is a strange anomaly that by the time Silver Patriarch retired to stud, St. Leger winners had completely lost favour with commercial flat breeders, yet Silver Patriarch has been one of the best patronised of all the many stallions to have stood at the National Stud in recent times and never seems to miss the opportunity of appearing at a stallion parade.

By far the most successful stallion for the National Stud since it moved to Newmarket was Mill Reef and it was from his owner-breeder, the American, Paul Mellon, that Peter Winfield acquired Silver Patriarch's dam, Early Rising. This grey mare, a relative of Mellon's US champions, Fort Marcy and Key to the Mint, cost $160,000 at the 1988 Keeneland Breeding Stock Sale – at home on the stud she became known as Freckles for obvious reasons.

The selection on behalf of a friend, Peter Winfield, was made jointly by Tony Lakin, well known as a veterinary surgeon for United Racecourses, and his wife, Sarah – she ran a small independent bloodstock agency at their Lower Combe Farm, Bramley, Surrey. Subsequently the Lakins moved lock, stock and barrel to White's Farm, Wisborough Green, West Sussex, not far from where Silver Patriarch was trained at Arundel by John Dunlop.

Peter Winfield, a retired chartered surveyor living in Kingston-upon-Thames, died in November 1999, by which time Silver Patriarch had concluded his racing career and, most generously, he bequeathed half of his homebred grey to the National Stud. At the time his dam had a colt by Singspiel in utero and the resulting foal, Papineau, won the 2004 Gold Cup at Royal Ascot for Godolphin, their fourth winner of the race in the space of nine years.

Reared at White's Farm, Papineau was sold to Sheikh Mohammed as a foal for 85,000 guineas and the Lakins were underbidders. "Peter left us the mare, but not the foal she was carrying," explains Tony Lakin. "I was asked if I would mind taking the mare over technically one minute after he was foaled." Early Rising's only subsequent (living) foal, a grey own-sister to Papineau born in 2003, has been retained and is named Summer's Eve.

Silver Patriarch's St. Leger victory, which provided Pat Eddery with the 4,000th winner of his career, was marvellous compensation for the colt's short head defeat by Benny The Dip in the Derby – had he prevailed at Epsom, he would have been the first grey to win the Blue Riband since Airborne in 1946. Back at Epsom as a four-year-old to land the Coronation Cup, the grey gained another Group 1 victory in Italy.

Silver Patriarch has been promoted by the National Stud (sponsors of the 'Silver Patriarch Handicap 'Chase at Fakenham), as a dual purpose stallion, but his future surely lies as a jumping sire. In fact he had his very first winner, over hurdles at Folkestone in November 2004, just days before his first flat winner, the grey Party Boss, on the all-weather at Southwell.

SLEEPING PARTNER

Grey, 1966, by Parthia - Old Dutch

Owner: 6th Earl of Rosebery
Trainer: Doug Smith
Jockey: John Gorton
Breeder: 6th Earl of Rosebery

It was a poignant occasion for 87-year-old Lord Rosebery as he stood in the winner's enclosure at Epsom after his homebred grey Sleeping Partner had triumphed in the 1969 Oaks.

In that hallowed enclosure Harry Rosebery recalled how Sir Jack Jarvis, his trainer for over half a century, had forecast her Oaks victory in their last telephone conversation the previous December, not long before the great Newmarket trainer died – it was an unlikely prediction considering that the filly's solitary success from seven juvenile starts had been in a maiden at the Ayr Western Meeting in September, one of her owner-breeder's favourite venues.

Certainly the grand old man of the Turf would have taken it all with a pinch of salt – indeed he must have despaired of ever having an Oaks winner for his famous primrose and rose hoops had already finished second four times and third twice in the fillies' premier classic – he had won all the colts' classics, so his belated Oaks victory had a special significance.

Conversely, the success of Sleeping Partner provided a marvellous start to Rosebery's association with his new trainer, Doug Smith. At that time the former champion jockey presided over two establishments in Newmarket, Loder Stables, where he had embarked upon his training career the previous season, and Jack Jarvis' former yard, Park Lodge.

All Rosebery's horses, including Sleeping Partner, were based at Park Lodge, their day-to-day supervision being in the hands of Doug Smith's newly appointed assistant, Michael Stoute. The week after Sleeping Partner's classic victory, Michael got married when some wag sent a greetings telegram that read, 'What a lucky man to have two sleeping partners in a week!'

Surprisingly the first filly to complete the Lingfield Oaks Trial Stakes and Oaks double, Sleeping Partner went on to complete the hat-trick in the Ribblesdale Stakes, but she was afflicted by the cough soon afterwards and never recaptured her form albeit she remained in training the following season.

Bred at her owner's famous Mentmore Stud on heavy clay land in the Whaddon country in Buckinghamshire, the Oaks heroine owed her light grey coat to her dam, Old Dutch. She in turn had inherited it from her sire, Fastnet Rock, who was by Blue Peter's son, Ocean Swell. Like Blue Peter and Ocean Swell, Harry Rosebery's two homebred Derby winners, Fastnet Rock was a Mentmore-based stallion.

One aspect of Lord Rosebery's long-term involvement with the Turf for which he will always be remembered was a flair for naming his horses. One filly by Ocean Swell out of Model he famously called Bra – quite a risqué name back in the 1950s for a one-time Secretary of State for Scotland!

Sleeping Partner might have afforded a few inspired naming opportunities, but for the fact that she never had a live foal. Indeed the writing was on the wall by the time her owner-breeder died at Mentmore in May 1974.

Foaled at Egerton Stud where her dam was visiting Abernant, Sleeping Partner was a rarity amongst Thoroughbreds as Bill Cornish, one of the most experienced stud grooms, explains "She was the only foal that I have ever seen who was actually born grey."

SOVEREIGN PATH

Grey, 1956, by Grey Sovereign - Mountain Path

Owner: Ron Mason
Trainer: Ron Mason
Jockeys: Harry Carr, Lester Piggott
Breeder: Archie McIntyre

A haulage contractor and former speedway rider at Manchester's Bell View track, Ron Mason was also a highly successful owner, trainer and breeder based at his Guilsborough Hall home, about ten miles north of Northampton, before he decided to emigrate to Australia.

During the comparatively short time that he held a trainer's licence, he owned two outstanding milers in Sovereign Path and Track Spare, respective winners of the Queen Elizabeth II Stakes and the St. James's Palace Stakes – Track Spare earned a unique distinction at Newmarket in 1965 by winning the first race in Great Britain started from stalls.

Traditionally these two prestigious races are both run at Ascot, but Sovereign Path's Queen Elizabeth II Stakes was held at Newbury, where he also won the Lockinge Stakes, yet another event which now carries Group 1 status. Placed in numerous other top races, his Queen Elizabeth victory was fortuitous as that great grey filly, Petite Etoile, was a last minute absentee through coughing.

Initially, Sovereign Path, who had cost 700 guineas as a yearling at Doncaster from Theakston Stud, near Bedale, in Yorkshire, where he was bred, was trained in Ireland by Aubrey Brabazon – he and Ron Mason had met when the latter, then a Dublin-based car salesman, attended an Irish race meeting in order to sell a vehicle to the former Irish champion National Hunt jockey.

Whilst with Aubrey Brabazon the grey was an appropriate winner of The Tetrarch Stakes for three-year-olds on his local Curragh course. Later that season his owner took out a licence to train himself whereupon the colt was transferred to his own training quarters in Northamptonshire.

The son of Grey Sovereign returned to Ireland to stand at Terence Vigors' Burgage Stud, Co. Carlow. Tel Vigors later moved to what is now Kingwood Stud, Lambourn, to be near his son, Nicky, then training in Upper Lambourn. It was Tel's younger brother, Tim, who laid the foundations of the vast Coolmore enterprise in Ireland. But Burgage has a totally unexpected claim to fame for it was here that the hymn, 'All things bright and beautiful, all creatures great and small' first saw the light of day.

Although Sovereign Path was notably straight in front, a conformation defect that he transmitted to many of his offspring, he proved not only a prolific sire of winners, but also, more importantly in the long-term, a major sire of sires worldwide. Three of them, Supreme Sovereign (sire of Nocturnal Spree), Town Crier (sire of Cry of Truth), and Warpath, feature in this book.

So too does his outstanding daughter, Humble Duty, winner of the 1970 One Thousand Guineas. Two more of his grey daughters are Ron Mason's homebred, Petite Path, whom he saddled to win the Queen Mary Stakes and the Ayr Gold Cup, and Everything Nice, dam of Irish One Thousand Guineas winner, Nicer.

At the time when Sovereign Path was making his name as a stallion, many of his contemporaries succumbed to the enormous purchasing power of the yen. After the 1968 covering season, the syndicate that owned the twelve-year-old declined an offer of £120,000 from Japan, greatly in excess of the original syndication value of £48,000.

Based throughout his stallion innings at Burgage Stud, Sovereign Path had a fatal heart attack in December 1977, aged twenty-one – a long life but not as long as his own sire, Grey Sovereign.

STALBRIDGE COLONIST

Grey, 1959, by Colonist II - Eesofud

Owner: Ronald Blindell
Trainer: Ken Cundell
Jockey: Stan Mellor
Breeder: Harry Dufosee

To ensure that Stalbridge Colonist enjoyed a happy retirement, his breeder, Harry Dufosee, who had originally sold him privately as a four-year-old after he had won in the show ring, bought him back as a twelve-year-old for 680 guineas at the Ascot Sales in June 1971.

Following the death of shoe manufacturer, Ron Blindell, Stalbridge Colonist had realised 6,400 guineas in the same ring in December 1969. The grey had carried the colours of Plymouth Argyle Football Club of which his owner was chairman and he proved the best jumper trained by Ken Cundell at Roden House, Compton, in Berkshire, who was succeeded there by his son, Peter, former president of the National Trainers' Federation.

The son of Sir Winston's Churchill's popular grey Colonist II won sixteen races altogether of which twelve were 'chases. In 1966 he had become one of an elite few to beat the mighty Arkle over fences when depriving that great champion of a third successive victory in the Hennessy Cognac Gold Cup at Newbury, albeit in receipt of 35lbs. On the run-in, Stan Mellor galvanized the 25-1 outsider in a field of six to get up and win by half a length.

Two more of his most important victories were achieved at Sandown Park, in the Mildmay Memorial 'Chase and the Gainsborough 'Chase. A fine staying 'chaser, he was also placed in successive Cheltenham Gold Cups, finishing second to Woodland Venture, beaten three quarters of a length, and third to Fort Leney and The Laird, beaten a neck and a length.

The gelding was a great grandson of May Bush whom Lord Stalbridge had given as a present to Harry Dufosee. At the time he was agent for the Stalbridge Estate, near Sturminster Newton, in Dorset, including Stalbridge Park, which subsequently became Dufosee's own property.

Both Hugh Stalbridge and Harry Dufosee were stalwarts when it came to breeding jumpers – more recently part of the land at Stalbridge has been owned by local timber merchant, John Turner, breeder of a very different star in 1997 July Cup hero, Compton Place, now standing at Whitsbury Manor Stud.

Stalbridge Colonist was out of Eesofud, who is also the dam of Domason, winner of the 1970 National Hunt 'Chase, a race the Dufosees had always wanted to win. Eesofud (Dufosee spelt backwards), was a name chosen after three other suggestions to Weatherbys were rejected. Other descendants of May Bush include the multiple winners, Stalbridge Park (half-sister to Eesofud), Bantry Bay and Spring Corn, dam of 1969 Cheltenham Gold Cup runner-up, Domacorn.

Harry Dufosee, whose forebears were Huguenots, was eighty-six when he predeceased Stalbridge Colonist in May, 1976, but only weeks before he had made provision for the grey's final years by entrusting him to his friends, Bobby and Barbara Bowen at Emborough, near Shepton Mallet.

Both Lord Stalbridge and Harry Dufosee have 'chases named after them on the Boxing Day card at Wincanton. But for Harry Dufosee's support along with other farming colleagues, their local course, where Stalbridge Colonist won his first race over hurdles when trained by Tommy Jarvis in Devon, would not have survived after the war.

SUN CAP

Grey, 1951, by Sunny Boy III - Cappellina

Owner: Mme Robert Forget
Trainer: Reginald Carver
Jockey: Rae Johnstone
Breeder: Robert Forget

At a time when Gallic invaders dominated the English classics, Sun Cap crossed the Channel in 1954 and, adorned with a chic sheepskin noseband, she took the Oaks by six lengths from Altana and Philante, two other fillies likewise owned, trained and bred in France.

A workmanlike grey and rather light of bone, Sun Cap, who was a notoriously lazy worker on the home gallops at Chantilly, was slowly into her stride at Epsom but, after holding a prominent position at Tattenham Corner, she came wide on the outside down the straight to positively annihilate the opposition. Reginald Carver's first ever runner in England, the filly actually ran in borrowed colours.

A third Oaks winner for the Australian jockey, Rae Johnstone, who was based in France, Sun Cap had failed to score in four juvenile outings, and she started at 100-8 at Epsom despite victory in the Prix Penelope at Saint-Cloud in April. That was to prove her only other success – she was subsequently unplaced in both the Grand Prix de Paris and the Prix de l'Arc de Triomphe.

That year's 'Arc was won by another of Sunny Boy's offspring, Sica Boy, who was destined to become a stallion at William Hill's Whitsbury Stud in Hampshire. At the end of that season, Sunny Boy, who was homebred by Sun Cap's breeder, Robert Forget, and stood at his Haras du Verbois in Normandy, was syndicated under the management of Prince Aly Khan.

Sunny Boy was one of those rare stallions who seemed able to sire runners who were greatly superior to himself and the credit for Sun Cap's ability was probably owed much more to him than her dam, Cappellina – she ran for four seasons, winning two small races from thirty-three starts. Her dam, Bellina, was another grey, but was described erroneously as bay in the French Stud Book.

At the end of her three-year-old season, Sun Cap was purchased by Catherine Macdonald-Buchanan for her powerful Lavington, Lordship and Egerton Studs. However, she proved a disappointing broodmare, although one of her sons, In The Gloaming, made his mark as a sire in Argentina – her only daughter, Welsh Bonnet, was unraced through injury and made no worthwhile contribution at stud.

Thus Sun Cap set the precedent for the only other grey Oaks winners of the 20th century, as both Petite Etoile and Sleeping Partner had correspondingly disappointing stud careers.

Of course hopes had been high that Sun Cap would emulate the 1931 Oaks winner, Brulette, whom Catherine Macdonald-Buchanan's father, the one and only Lord Woolavington, had acquired for his Lavington Stud. Likewise bred and trained in France, she excelled in the paddocks and is ancestress of the outstanding 'Arc hero, Vaguely Noble.

SUNBITTERN

Grey, 1970, by Sea Hawk II - Pantoufle

Owner: Sir Thomas Pilkington, Bart
Trainer: Bruce Hobbs
Jockey: John Gorton
Breeder: Stackallan Stud

Some indication of Sunbittern's prowess as a foundation mare is afforded by the fact that in 2005 she featured as the third dam of the One Thousand Guineas heroine, Virginia Waters, and the fourth dam of the Irish Two Thousand Guineas winner, Dubawi.

Sunbittern herself was at her most uncooperative as a three-year-old – at Goodwood in May she unseated her rider at the start and at Epsom on Derby Day she refused to race. It was all the more disappointing for as a juvenile she had won her first three outings before finishing fourth to her brilliant stable-companion, Jacinth, in the Cheveley Park Stakes.

Trained by Bruce Hobbs, who famously won the 1938 Grand National aged seventeen on Battleship and is the trainer of another star of *Grey Magic* in Cry of Truth, Sunbittern was invariably ridden by stable jockey, John Gorton, the South African who was also associated with the grey Oaks heroine, Sleeping Partner.

Sunbittern's immediate background involves two families linked indelibly by marriage. Although both have their origins in England, their major contribution as bloodstock breeders has been in Ireland.

Sunbittern was bred by Liz Burke of Stackallan (later spelt Stackallen) Stud, Co. Meath, whose daughter, Sonia, was married to the late Tim Rogers. He stood the sire, Sea Hawk II (also sire of *Grey Magic* celebrities, Erimo Hawk and Bruni) at his Airlie Stud. Co. Dublin; and the grey filly carried the red and green colours of Sonia's brother, Tommy Pilkington.

A former senior steward of the Jockey Club, Sir Thomas Henry Milborne-Swinnerton-Pilkington is the 14th baronet, a title conferred upon an ancestor for supporting King Charles I against Oliver Cromwell. Tommy, who lives in a neo-Venetian house, Kings Walden, near Hitchin, in Hertfordshire, designed by Quinlan Terry, knows his roots, "We're landowners from Yorkshire, the glass Pilkingtons are from Lancashire."

Sunbittern's prowess as a broodmare stems principally from three daughters, two of whom are greys – Seriema, is the dam of Infamy, winner of the Rothmans' International at Woodbine in Canada for Gerald Leigh whose celebrated broodmare, Canton Silk, also features in *Grey Magic*.

Another grey daughter of Sunbittern, High Tern enjoyed a brilliant classic double in the summer of 1998 when her son, High-Rise, won the Derby and her grand-daughter, Zomaradah, won the Italian Oaks; the latter is the dam of Dubawi.

High Tern cost Sheikh Mohammed 420,000 guineas as a yearling as that year her half-sister, High Hawk, had been running up a sequence of Group victories. The latter's son, In The Wings, won the Breeders' Cup Turf, Belmont Park, and became a leading sire at the Sheikh's Kildangan Stud, Co. Kildare, where he died in 2004.

When High-Rise was a yearling, Sheikh Mohammed sold his dam, High Tern, as a barren mare for 6,500 guineas – two years after High-Rise won the Derby, her new owners of whom Tommy Pilkington's son, Richard, was one, sold a yearling half-brother for 125,000 guineas.

SUNY BAY

Grey, 1989, by Roselier - Suny Salome

Owner: Uplands Bloodstock
Trainers: Charlie Brooks, Simon Sherwood
Jockey: Graham Bradley
Breeder: Mrs. E.M. Codd

All the jumpers included in *Grey Magic* are featured because of their most famous victory or victories with the exception of Suny Bay – he is there primarily on account of two magnificent defeats when finishing runner-up in consecutive Grand Nationals during the 'nineties, ridden first by Jamie Osborne and then by his regular partner, Graham Bradley.

An outstanding staying 'chaser, he is the best horse to have carried the distinctive blue colours with white stars of Uplands Bloodstock, the racing alias of Andrew Cohen. Founder of the Betterware catalogue business, he bought the Uplands yard in Upper Lambourn from Charlie Brooks who had previously been Fred Winter's assistant there.

Like so many top 'chasers, Suny Bay was bought from that master purveyor of jumpers, Tom Costello, in Ireland. Andrew Cohen relates, "We could not agree over a price for a batch of four and Tom said he would include this grey in the deal provided I left him there to pursue a point-to-point career in Ireland at his expense. And first time out he got beaten a short-head by Ask Tom who became a champion two-mile 'chaser."

The grey Roselier gelding did win an Irish point-to-point before coming to England to join John Upson, near Towcester, but following his owner's purchase of Uplands, he was then transferred to Charlie Brooks. Uplands is adjacent to Saxon House where Fulke Walwyn trained the grey's maternal grandsire, Sunyboy – he provided The Queen Mother with her 300th victory under National Hunt Rules.

During the course of his career in England, Suny Bay became one of the most popular 'chasers of his generation, winning ten races over fences highlighted by the Hennessy Cognac Gold Cup as an eight-year-old. Along with One Man, Teeton Mill and What's Up Boys, he was one of four greys to win the Newbury spectacular within the space of seven years – One Man was another Tom Costello graduate.

Suny Bay's 1997 Hennessy victory was sandwiched between two gallant seconds in the Grand National – first behind Lord Gyllene and then to Earth Summit. On the latter occasion he gave one of the finest weight carrying performances of modern times. Putting up a superb display of jumping in the bottomless ground with top-weight of 12st, he was trying to concede the winner 23lbs.

His aptitude for jumping the Aintree fences, where he completed the course four times, was not surprising as he also loved the formidable obstacles at Haydock Park, winning no fewer than four graded events there, the Edward Hanmer Memorial 'Chase, twice, the Tommy Whittle 'Chase and the Greenalls Grand National Trial.

For an interim period Suny Bay was trained by Charlie Brooks' successor at Uplands, Simon Sherwood, but then Andrew Cohen sold Uplands and established his own private training stables at Wood Hall Stud, Shenley, in Hertfordshire, presided over by Alex Hales. The grey was then twelve years of age and, after being pulled up in four of his last seven starts, he was retired to become his trainer's hack.

SUPREME SOVEREIGN

Grey, 1964, by Sovereign Path - Valtellina

Owner: Mrs. Henry Hodges
Trainer: Harry Wragg
Jockey: Ron Hutchinson
Breeder: William Mitchell

Beware this horse is dangerous: only authorised persons to handle this horse, proclaimed the huge notice which hung outside Supreme Sovereign's box in the 1970s at the Muir family's Fawley Stud, next to Whatcombe, on the Oxfordshire/Berkshire borders.

Ian Muir, whose expertise with difficult stallions was part of stud folklore, stood Supreme Sovereign, winner of the Lockinge Stakes as a four-year-old, for four seasons – he arrived at Fawley from Bourton Hill Stud, at Sezincote, in the Cotswolds, having stood previously at various locations in Ireland. While based at Corbally Stud, Co. Kildare, he actually mauled someone, breaking their arm and three ribs in the process.

Silver, as he was known at Fawley, had the deserved reputation as a savage. He would strike out, bear his teeth and roar like a lion when approached. However, it soon became apparent that he was terrified of water and so long as one was carrying a full bucket he would beat a retreat. To give added protection, a semi circular wire-mesh barrier was erected around his stable door, with free access to a paddock behind with an ingenious chute to enable him to cover his mares. Immediately after covering he would thrust his head out, half close his eyes and tremble all over. He refused to be shod by the farrier and in the end his hooves were kept trimmed by using an electric grinder. He also loved those sweets known as 'jelly-babies', but only the black variety, which his owner's husband used to send, 10lbs at a time, on a regular basis from the safety of their home in Sheffield.

In 1979 the stallion was sold to Hungary. Against all the odds, the three-day journey by horsebox to just north of Budapest was completed without incident despite the fact that he was accompanied by two broodmares. He actually covered a mare the day after his arrival and soon he had befriended an Alsatian bitch – amazingly she would lie on his manger, undisturbed, while he ate.

Sadly, Supreme Sovereign died two years later. Quite a successful sire despite his temperament and erratic fertility, his most noted offspring was the grey 1975 One Thousand Guineas heroine, Nocturnal Spree, but he will always be remembered as 'jaws' in terms of contemporary Thoroughbred stallions.

It is probably indicative of his character that the horse had a different handler in all three of his seasons' in training, at two with Vic Mitchell at Malton, at three with Avril Vasey at Middleham, and at four with Harry Wragg at Newmarket. His owner purchased him originally as a yearling for 6,100 guineas at Tattersalls' Houghton Sales from Collinstown Stud, Co. Kildare, owned by William Mitchell, whose nephew, Philip, is responsible for running Prince Khalid Abdullah's Juddmonte Farms.

Another smart grey to retire to stand at Fawley Stud was Jellaby and he too should have won the Lockinge Stakes. Deemed the most unlucky loser of 1978, this grandson of Palestine had an unassailable lead when he stumbled and dislodged his jockey about a hundred yards from the winning post.

TAGALIE

Grey, 1909, by Cyllene - Tagale

Owner: Walter Raphael
Trainer: Dawson Waugh
Jockeys: Johnny Reiff, Leslie Hewitt
Breeder: Walter Raphael

One of only three greys to win the Derby during the 20th century along with Mahmoud and Airborne, Walter Raphael's homebred Tagalie is the only grey filly ever to win the Blue Riband despite being slight of stature and noticeably back at the knee with a decidedly delicate constitution.

A Jewish financier of Dutch extraction, Walter Raphael employed Dawson Waugh as his private trainer at Somerville Lodge, Newmarket (the yard from which William Haggas dispatched Shaamit to win the 1996 Derby), and Tagalie provided them with their first classic success when she triumphed in the 1912 One Thousand Guineas prior to her sensational all the way victory in the Derby – she was the first grey to win the Newmarket classic since its inauguration nearly 100 years earlier.

Two days after the Derby, she turned out again for the Oaks, but with odds of 2-1 laid on was unplaced, having not been allowed to bowl along in front as was her custom. It was then felt that a fortnight's holiday exercising in the sea off the Norfolk coast might prove beneficial but, notwithstanding this seasonal break, she was unplaced on her remaining two starts, the Eclipse Stakes and the St. Leger.

Bred in Ireland where Walter Raphael boarded his mares on a farm bordering the Curragh, Tagalie was foaled in 1909. That season the same owner-trainer combination had been represented by the Derby runner-up, Louviers, although many observers were convinced that the short head verdict in favour of King Edward VII's Minoru should have gone the other way.

Conversely nearly everyone thought that Louviers' own-brother, Louvois, had been beaten by Craganour in the 1913 Two Thousand Guineas only to be announced the winner; then Craganour finished first in the Derby, only to be disqualified in favour of the runner-up, Aboyeur, with Louvois promoted from third place to second.

Both Tagalie and Louvois were ridden by Johnny Reiff who by that time was based in France. Johnny and his elder brother, Lester, had come to England from the USA to ride for a nucleus of unsavoury American gamblers who had perfected the art of doping towards the end of the 19th century. Dressed in Eton collars and knickerbockers and with the fresh complexion of youth, the brothers resembled innocent choirboys, but in effect they were bent on carrying out the instructions of their unscrupulous employers. Their departure to France had been precipitated when Lester Reiff had been warned off by the Jockey Club – the stewards were dissatisfied with his riding of a horse at Manchester in September, 1901, when in a driving finish he succumbed by a head to his brother.

Tagalie's distaff pedigree lent little encouragement as a future classic winner although her half-brother, Blankney II, had won the 1908 Gimcrack Stakes for Walter Raphael. Before he bought their dam, Tagale, in France, she had been claimed as a two-year-old for £600 after winning at Chantilly. One of Tagalie's sons, Tagrag, sired that notable grey sprinter, Tag End.

TAG END

Grey, 1924, by Tagrag - Short Line

Owner: Jack Joel
Trainer: Charles Peck
Jockeys: Brownie Carslake, Freddie Fox, Harry Wragg
Breeder: M. Kavanagh

Although Jack Joel's famous Childwick Bury Stud, near St. Albans, in Hertfordshire, was by then on the wane as a nursery for potential classic winners, what induced him to buy the sprinter, Tag End, towards the end of his three-year-old career after he had won five consecutive races in his native Ireland, is uncertain. Perhaps he wanted a horse to compete with his wife's smart sprinter, Polar Bear.

In some respects the purchase from Harry Ussher, one of the first significant deals negotiated by that doyen of Irish bloodstock agents, Bertie Kerr, was reminiscent of the top-class sprinter, Song, whom Jack Joel's son, Jim, bought many years later whilst in training. However, he had considerable value as an entire – there were no stallion prospects for Tag End as he had been gelded before he ever set foot on a racecourse.

Transferred to Jack Joel's private trainer, Charles Peck, who by then had moved from Wantage to Foxhill in Wiltshire, on the other side of the Lambourn Downs, Tag End began inauspiciously for his new connections – he swerved at the old barrier start for the Molyneux Cup at Liverpool, thus forfeiting whatever chance he may have had, but he was to win the race the following season.

In each of the next two seasons (1928/29) he won both the Portland Handicap and the Nunthorpe Stakes, and went on to win a third consecutive Nunthorpe Stakes as a six-year-old. The intermediate Nunthorpe produced a memorable finish between two greys as Royal Minstrel, at 3-1 on, succumbed by a neck.

In 1929 the old gelding was ridden by Freddie Fox at Doncaster and York and by Harry Wragg when winning the King's Stand Stakes, as his regular partner, Brownie Carslake, had temporarily forsaken the saddle to try his hand at training. But the Australian was to be reunited with him for the last of his twenty victories, at Sandown Park as a nine-year-old. It was Brownie Carslake who had ridden the grey Tetratema to win the 1920 Two Thousand Guineas.

Few racehorses prove superior to their own sires, but Tag End was a notable exception. He belonged to the first crop of Tagrag, who won a clutch of insignificant races. The last of two successes at Epsom on Derby Day came aged eight after which he was sold at Tattersalls' December Sales for 320 guineas to the Jacob brothers.

Tagrag was retained for the duration of his stallion career which was spent in Ireland at Enniscorthy, Co. Wexford, where he died in 1937. Although only really a selling plater, he was a well bred one, by Chaucer out of the illustrious Tagalie, another celebrity featured in *Grey Magic*.

TAJ MAH

Grey, 1926, by Lemberg - Taj Mahal

Owner: Simon Guthmann
Trainer: John Torterolo
Jockey: Wally Sibbritt
Breeder: H.H. Aga Khan III

There was a certain irony about the Deauville sales in 1927. The Aga Khan, who had spent a fortune on yearlings in his relentless quest for classic winners, consigned his first ever draft of yearlings and they included Ukrania, who proceeded to win the French Oaks, and Taj Mah, winner of the One Thousand Guineas.

Taj Mah was purchased for 250,000fr (about £2,000) by Simon Guthmann, who came from Alsace, and sent to be trained by John Torterolo, a native of Uruguay, who had been a leading trainer in Argentina, before moving to Lamorlaye in France. A diminutive grey measuring barely 15 hands, Taj Mah won three modest races at Deauville (worth little over £100 apiece) from five juvenile starts.

Although looking as though she did not stay 6 furlongs on her seasonal finale in the Criterium de Maisons-Laffitte, Simon Guthmann was determined to let his grey take her chance in the One Thousand Guineas, much to the dismay of her trainer – evidently just before leaving home for Newmarket John Torterolo told his brother that he would willingly give £100 to be spared such an unnecessary journey.

Certainly the portents were not very favourable – after a poor Channel crossing, the filly was off her feed on arriving in

Newmarket. On the day the combined pessimism of both trainer and jockey finally undermined the owner's confidence. He had telephoned his London office from Paris asking for £300 to be delivered to the London hotel at which he was staying with the intention of having £100 each-way on his filly. In the event he speculated just £15 and, if he took starting price, he obtained 33-1 to his money.

Successful by three-parts of a length at Newmarket from the joint-favourite, Sister Anne, Taj Mah never ran again and her owner immediately sent her to visit his own grey stallion, Biribi, at Haras de la Pomme (later owned by Tony Richards of Ewar Stud Farms). Winner of the Prix de l'Arc de Triomphe ridden by John Torterolo's son, Domingo, Biribi was champion sire in France in 1941.

Taj Mah was Taj Mahal's initial offspring and was foaled in England at Harwood Stud, when her dam was visiting Gainsborough, after whom Sheikh Maktoum Al Maktoum's stud near Newbury is now named. Taj Mahal inherited her grey coat from her sire, The Tetrarch, and she was bred by the latter's trainer, Atty Persse, but she won for the Aga Khan, who bought her as a yearling at Newmarket for 1,600 guineas when consigned from Moyglare Stud, Co. Kildare.

TEETON MILL

Grey, 1989, by Neltino - Celtic Well

Owner: The Winning Line
Trainer: Venetia Williams
Jockey: Norman Williamson
Breeder: Kathleen Hayward

The irrepressible Desert Orchid heralded a galaxy of grey jumping stars in the 1990s and one that looked set to shine as brightly as any was Teeton Mill, a wonderful flagship horse for The Winning Line syndicate.

Like another celebrated grey, One Man, Teeton Mill graduated from the hunting field as have many jumping stars in the past, but whereas the former came from Ireland the latter was bred and raised in the Heart of England, in the vicinity of Teeton Mill in the Pytchley country.

When Teeton Mill gained his first major victory under Rules at the advanced age of nine in the 1998 Hennessy Cognac Gold Cup, he was taking his record to seven wins from eight starts over fences – he had concluded his exploits in hunter-chases by landing the Horse & Hound Cup at Stratford-upon-Avon; earlier he had won three point-to-points.

His commanding victory at Newbury by fifteen lengths suggested that Herefordshire trainer, Venetia Williams, had an obvious Gold Cup contender on her hands, a view endorsed when he won both the King George VI 'Chase at Kempton Park on Boxing Day and the Ascot 'Chase in February in the most convincing fashion from his grey contemporary, Senor El Betrutti. The latter event was a substitute for the Pillar 'Chase at

Cheltenham, which he missed due to a bruised foot and slight muscle problems.

His victory in the 'King George' was the seventh time that a grey had won this feature event in a twelve-year period, while the success of What's Up Boys in the 2001 'Hennessy' was the fourth time that a grey had won in the space of seven years – remarkable figures to say the least.

Teeton Mill started second favourite to Florida Pearl for the 1999 Cheltenham Gold Cup, but was pulled up before half-way – early in the race he sustained a serious tendon injury to his off-hind hock. After a year's rest and recuperation he went back into training, but he never recaptured his sparkle at Kings Caple and it was finally decided to retire him to the hunting field – an anti-climax to a belated career that had promised so much.

By Further Flight's half-brother, Neltino, whom Lady Beaverbrook stood at The Elms Stud, where he covered free of charge initially, he was bred by Kathleen Hayward – her family had procured his third dam, Arceeno, back in the 1950s and Teeton Mill's dam, Celtic Well, was an own-sister to the top-class, but ill-fated hurdler, Celtic Ryde. Arceeno's racing career came to a premature halt when she fell at Warwick, ran loose into the town and injured herself.

Mrs Hayward's daughter, Janet, recalls the original purchase of Arceeno. "One day Frank Cundell telephoned my father to say that one of his owners could not pay his bill for training Arceeno and he recommended that he bought her. At the time father had a number of flat mares, so he persuaded my mother to buy her instead."

Also closely involved with Teeton Mill was Dick Saunders, the amateur rider who rode Grittar to victory in the 1982 Grand National, and his daughter, Caroline Bailey – she runs one of the country's most successful point-to-point yards at Spratton in Northamptonshire. He originally bought Teeton Mill as a foal and she supervised his formative years and introduced the grey to racing between the flags.

TERIMON

Grey, 1986, by Bustino - Nicholas Grey

Owner: Marcia, Lady Beaverbrook
Trainer: Clive Brittain
Jockey: Michael Roberts
Breeder: Hesmonds Stud Ltd.

When Lady Beaverbrook's grey Terimon finished second to Nashwan in the 1989 Derby at odds of 500-1, he became the longest priced runner to finish in the frame in the long and colourful history of the Blue Riband of the Turf.

There was a certain irony about the result as Nashwan was trained by Dick Hern at West Ilsley. He had trained Terimon's sire, Bustino, for Lady B, just about the biggest investor in the yearling market prior to the Arabs, until they had a disagreement and she gradually transferred her horses to Clive Brittain at Newmarket.

Terimon went on to win the International Stakes at York as a five-year-old, beating the previous year's Derby winner, Quest For Fame. With additional Group 1 placings, including third in the Coronation Cup as a six-year-old, he more than justified the 140,000 guineas he had cost when consigned from Hesmonds Stud in East Sussex at Tattersalls' October Yearling Sales, the highest price of the week, a reflection on his good looks rather than his pedigree.

Hesmonds Stud is owned by Greek shipping magnate, Peter Goulandris, and Lady B was born Marcia Anastasia Christoforides, daughter of a tobacco merchant of Cypriot extraction. She was married briefly to two enormously rich

Canadian entrepreneurs; first Sir James Dunn, chairman of the Algoma Steel Corporation, whose fortune enabled her to pursue her extensive racing interests, and then Lord Beaverbrook, proprietor of the *Daily Express*.

In the early days, Sir Gordon Richards acted as Lady B's racing manager, but subsequently she relied a good deal on Newmarket veterinary surgeon, Bob Crowhurst, and his son-in-law, Joss Collins, of the British Bloodstock Agency – he arranged for Terimon to retire to Lord Fairhaven's Barton Stud, near Bury St Edmunds, where he also acted as a consultant. The stud had been started in the 1920s by another newspaper mogul, Sir Edward Hulton.

A grand little horse of good conformation and a sweet nature, Terimon stood there alongside two other Beaverbrook flag-bearers in Mystiko, another grey featured in *Grey Magic*, and Charmer – their owner was always very concerned that all her horses should find good homes once they had retired from the racecourse. One of her all-time favourites was the gelded Boldboy, who spent his retirement at Sir John Astor's Warren Stud, Newmarket, where he was treated like a priceless stallion.

She was also very superstitious and, almost without exception, her horses had names of seven letters, her lucky number. Perhaps the best known was Terimon's own sire, Bustino. And if one of her horses happened to be number seven on the racecard that was regarded as a virtual guarantee of success!

Marcia Beaverbrook died in 1994 and later Terimon became a jumping sire at Shade Oak Stud in Shropshire. Another of her greys to make his mark in this sphere was The Elms Stud resident, Neltino, a half-brother to one distinguished grey in Further Flight, and sire of another in Teeton Mill. For the 2005 covering season, Terimon was joined by another grey in Fair Mix, a French-bred son of Linamix.

TETRATEMA

Grey, 1917, by The Tetrarch - Scotch Gift

Owner: Dermot McCalmont
Trainer: Atty Persse
Jockey: Brownie Carslake
Breeder: Dermot McCalmont

The uncertainty of breeding is well illustrated by the experiences of Dermot McCalmont. He had two homebred grey winners of the Two Thousand Guineas in The Tetrarch's son, Tetratema, and the latter's son, Mr. Jinks, both of them brilliant two-year-olds trained by Atty Persse at Stockbridge, in Hampshire, better known nowadays for trout fishing on the River Test.

In due course they retired to their owner's Ballylinch Stud, Co. Kilkenny, in Ireland. Whereas Tetratema emulated his own sire by becoming champion, Mr. Jinks made a very promising start at stud only to gradually fade from the scene into obscurity.

As a two-year-old, Tetratema had a comparable record to his illustrious sire, The Tetrarch, when both were undefeated and topped the Free Handicap. The former headed the weights with 9st 7lbs, by a record 12lbs, while the latter was allotted 3lbs more, 10lbs above his nearest adversary. The difference, of course, was that The Tetrarch never raced beyond his two-year-old days.

Tetratema, meanwhile, became a champion in each of the next two seasons. Following victories in the National Breeders' Produce Stakes, Molecomb Stakes, Champagne Stakes, Imperial Produce Plate and Middle Park Plate as a juvenile, he then triumphed in the Two Thousand Guineas. After exhibiting predictable stamina limitations in both the Derby and the Eclipse Stakes, he then won the King George Stakes. He repeated that Goodwood success the following season when he also won the King's Stand Stakes and July Cup – he was never beaten over sprint distances.

Amongst the top ten stallions in eleven seasons between the two World Wars, Tetratema was champion sire in 1929, the year that Mr. Jinks won the Two Thousand Guineas. From the same crop came the brilliant filly, Tiffin, who was the champion two-year-old of her generation and champion of her sex the following year – she was unbeaten in eight starts.

It was a red letter day for Tetratema when two of his progeny, Tiffin and Royal Minstrel, were locked together in a desperate finish for the July Cup, with victory going to the diminutive filly by a short head. Royal Minstrel is a *Grey Magic* celebrity as is Tetratema's daughter, Myrobella; and Tetratema is also the maternal grandsire of another in Palestine.

Many of Tetratema's progeny stayed better than he did and another classic winner was Four Course – a very smart juvenile winning the July Stakes, Richmond Stakes and Gimcrack Stakes, she proceeded to win the One Thousand Guineas and was only just beaten in the Oaks.

As The Tetrarch's most influential son, it was appropriate that Tetratema should have been buried alongside The Tetrarch at Ballylinch when he died in July 1939. It is Tetratema's grey own-brother, The Satrap, who was thought to be The Tetrarch's last living son; his death was recorded at the advanced age of twenty-seven in November 1951. Amongst The Satrap's progeny was the good stayer, Auralia, yet another grey.

THE CALLANT

Grey, 1948, by St. Michael - Windywalls

Owner: Charlie Scott
Trainer: Stewart Wight
Jockey: Jonathan Scott-Aiton
Breeder: Charlie Scott

There have been many celebrated 'chasers bred, reared and trained in the Scottish Lowlands and The Callant (a name derived from the Common Riding in this part of the country) was a grey, almost white, marauder of the 1950s, who twice crossed The Border to demolish his rivals at Cheltenham at what was then known as the National Hunt Meeting.

But first he proved himself in point-to-points in his native Scotland and the north of England. Carrying the colours of his owner-breeder, Charlie Scott, a farmer from Jedburgh, the son of St. Michael, a premium stallion for the Buccleuch Hunt, won all eight of his starts between the flags at the ages of six and seven.

The next stage of his career came about by accident rather than by design. Following his eighth successive victory, in the John Peel Cup at the Cumberland fixture, The Callant struck out while Charlie Scott was putting on his tail bandage. As the resulting injury involved a long convalescence for his handler, the grey gelding was sent to a professional trainer, Stewart Wight.

One of the country's leading National Hunt trainers, Stewart Wight was based at the remote outpost of Grantshouse, in Berwickshire. A trainer of the old school he was also a farmer and whether going racing or attending Edinburgh's Gorgie Market, he was never seen without his bowler hat and a carnation in his buttonhole.

The Callant made it thirteen wins from as many starts when winning the 1956 Foxhunters', but the sequence ended abruptly next time out when he blundered at the last fence when leading in a hunter 'chase at Ayr. The following season he won the Foxhunters' again in a memorable duel with the Australian Olympic horseman, Laurie Morgan, on Colledge Master, another great hunter-chaser. As usual the grey was ridden by Jimmy Scott-Aiton, also a Borders' farmer.

Many considered that The Callant could have won that year's Cheltenham Gold Cup had he been entered, but in truth he was never as good in open competition, although he won three 'chases during the 1957-58 season defeating, in turn, Much Obliged at Hexham, Kerstin at Ayr, and Wynburgh at Haydock Park. He also competed in the inaugural running of two famous 'chases. Uncharacteristically, he came to grief in the Whitbread Gold Cup (the first ever sponsored 'chase), running round bridleless afterwards, and was fourth in the Hennessy Cognac Gold Cup, then run at Cheltenham.

The Callant won sixteen 'chases and seventeen point-to-points. His first and last victories were at the Lauderdale fixture at Mosshouses – after a two years' absence from active competition, he won on his finale in 1960 ridden by his owner's fiancée, Rosie Bird. One of the great pointers of the post-war era, this family pet was never wrapped in cotton-wool and would do a full season's hunting with the Jedforest.

Charlie Scott's nephew, Peter Elliot, is still breeding successfully from the family up in the Cheviot Hills and he wore the same colours when beaten a short head in the 1970 Cheltenham Foxhunters' on homebred Jedheads, whose dam was an own-sister to The Callant.

An essential grey link in The Callant's pedigree is provided by the obscure Prince Philip. Not only was he a son of The Tetrarch's sire, Roi Hérode, but he was also homebred by The Tetrarch's breeder, Cub Kennedy, who stood him at Straffan Station Stud, Co. Kildare, at a fee of just 18 guineas.

THE TETRARCH

Grey, 1911, by Roi Hérode - Vahren

Owner: Dermot McCalmont
Trainer: Atty Persse
Jockey: Steve Donoghue
Breeder: Edward Kennedy

The whim of an Irish breeder was responsible for breeding The Tetrarch, the horse many regard as the fastest ever to grace the Turf. Furthermore he seemed to defy convention with regard to almost everything else about him, his unfashionable pedigree, his unorthodox stud record, but above all his exotic appearance. Indeed, he was a freak of the Thoroughbred species.

Edward Kennedy of Straffan Station Stud, Co. Kildare, had acquired the staying-bred Roi Hérode specifically to revive the male line of Hérod, notwithstanding that the grey was ten generations removed from that founding stallion. It was after finishing runner-up in the 1909 Doncaster Cup that the owner of Straffan Station purchased the French-bred for £2,000 and, when the horse broke down in training in England the following spring, he was retired to his stud in Ireland at a modest fee of 35 guineas.

By then it was late in the breeding season and one of the few mares Roi Hérode covered was Vahren, the winner of three small races whom Cub Kennedy had originally bought for £200. Previously a poor producer, she was fourteen when foaling The Tetrarch on April 22, 1911. It was not a formula that anyone in their wildest dreams could have envisaged breeding an outstanding racehorse, far less one with such phenomenal speed and precocity as The Tetrarch.

He was chesnut with black splotches when foaled, but by the

time he was a yearling and had already demonstrated his ability to outrun the deer in the park, the chesnut had turned to iron grey and the splotches to white – it really looked a though someone had splashed him all over with a bucket of whitewash. Although the colt was tall and ungainly, his owner was not to be deflected in his resolve to include him in his annual yearling consignment at Tattersalls' Doncaster Sales.

Atty Persse, an Irishman who trained at Chattis Hill, near Stockbridge, in Hampshire, had seen The Tetrarch at home prior to the sale and had taken a particular liking to the 'rocking horse,' as he was then dubbed, despite his untoward appearance. "The Tetrarch was one of the finest yearlings I ever saw," said Atty. "The chief impression he made on my mind was that he looked as though he owned the place. He had size and substance, and was a wonderful walker. I have never seen a horse that could get his hind legs so far in front of his forelegs. I was determined to buy him at Doncaster."

The Stockbridge trainer had a unique insight into the colt as he had actually trained his sire, Roi Hérode, for Cub Kennedy when he was transferred from France and, such was his speed, that Atty Persse considered him much more of a middle distance horse than a stayer. Furthermore he had trained The Tetrarch's elder half-sister, Nicola, winner of her solitary juvenile start – subsequently she herself was mated with Roi Hérode to produce the 1920 Coventry Stakes winner, the grey Milesius.

Second in a draft of seven lots sold by Cub Kennedy at Doncaster, the grey son of Roi Hérode and Vahren was the most expensive at 1,300 guineas. A week later, Atty Persse's cousin, Dermot McCalmont, arrived home from serving with the 7th Hussars in India. "I told him I had bought a really nice yearling and advised him to have it," Atty Persse recalled. "If he did not wish to take him altogether, I suggested that he should have a half share with me. Dermot had not seen the colt, but he promptly agreed to become the sole owner."

Before a year had elapsed, 'The Rocking Horse' had been

transformed into 'The Spotted Wonder', gaining such enormous public esteem that he would be cheered all the way down to the start – and his supporters were never disappointed.

Although rejected by most prospective purchasers at Doncaster as too big and coarse to make a racehorse, never mind a two-year-old, The Tetrarch proved remarkably easy to break in and he seemed to know exactly what to do just as soon as he was tacked up. Atty Persse's stable jockey, Steve Donoghue, who was to ride him in all his races and much of his work, always maintained that he had done it all before, and that it was "his second time on earth."

Atty was a past master at winning with two-year-olds first time out and his technique revolved around searching trials at home before they ever set foot on a racecourse. Much to his trainer's surprise The Tetrarch not only proved well forward in the spring of his two-year-old career, but he also put up some home trials ridden by Steve Donoghue which simply defied belief.

One particular trial with Dermot McCalmont's Captain Symons, a seven-year-old entire, occurred on April 12, before The Tetrarch was effectively two years of age. The Tetrarch, carrying 9st, gave the older horse a stone and won in a common canter – and according to the weight-for-age scale, Captain Symons had no less than 4st 5lbs in hand. Within a month Captain Symons had won a handicap at Chester from a three-year-old to whom he was conceding 19lbs.

Such was the standard of discipline and security at Chattis Hill that The Tetrarch was allowed to start at 5-1 on his début at the Newmarket Craven Meeting. To those in the know he must have been the biggest certainty of all time and he won like one scoring by four lengths in a field of twenty-one runners – it was the first of an almost uninterrupted sequence of wide margin, pillar to post, victories. He simply spread-eagled the opposition in the first couple of furlongs and the result was soon a fait accompli.

After Newmarket, he won in succession the Woodcote Stakes, Epsom, Coventry Stakes, Ascot Heath, National Breeders'

Produce Stakes, Sandown Park, Rous Memorial Stakes, Goodwood, Champion Breeders' Foal Stakes, Derby, and Champagne Stakes, Doncaster – he was the outstanding horse ever to run at Derby which was closed in 1939 and is now the county cricket ground. In only one of those races was the outcome ever in doubt. At Sandown, he nearly collided with the tapes and forfeited so much ground at the start that his cause looked hopeless, yet he still managed to get up and win by a neck.

The crowd had come to Esher that afternoon specifically to see this wonder horse, but they were blissfully unaware that the grey very nearly did not run. On being refused an additional complimentary badge for a friend, Dermot McCalmont threatened to withdraw his colt and but for the timely intervention of his trainer, he would undoubtedly have done so. In protest at such cavalier treatment, he promptly transferred his racing account from Messrs. Weatherbys to their then rivals, Messrs. Pratt.

It had been the intention to run The Tetrarch in the Imperial Produce Stakes, Kempton Park, in October, but a few days before the race he rapped his off-fore fetlock in a gallop and it was decided to retire him for the season; as a precautionary measure the joint was pin-fired that autumn. Thereafter he wore brushing boots for added protection and was specially shod, all of which helped to fuel the rumours that he was suffering from a variety of complaints including water on the knee!

Allotted top-weight of 9st 10lbs in the Free Handicap, 10lbs more than his closest adversary, the striking grey went into winter quarters at Chattis Hill as ante-post favourite for both the Two Thousand Guineas and the Derby and his owner, Dermot McCalmont, never gave serious consideration to an offer of £100,000 for his unbeaten colt.

How could anyone contemplate defeat for such a wonder horse? The first indication that all was not well came with the announcement that spring, which was an unduly wet one, that the colt was not as comparatively fit at that stage as he had been twelve months previously and consequently he would be an absentee from the Newmarket classic.

Thus his preparation focused on the Derby, but then disaster struck. Following a half-speed gallop some two weeks before Epsom, he pulled up lame and it transpired that he had aggravated the old injury to his off-fore – in striking the suspensory ligament he had ruptured the sheath of his tendon. It was an injury for which his trainer had always been prepared. In his slower paces the colt tended to plait his forelegs, crossing one in front of the other, so that the danger of a self inflicted injury was always present.

So ended The Tetrarch's sensational racing career, with the million dollar question remaining unanswered – would he or would he not have stayed one-and-a-half miles? Unfortunately the two men who knew the horse best had diverging views. Atty Persse said, "I honestly don't think he would ever have been beaten, at any distance. He was a freak and there will never be another like him." Steve Donoghue was more circumspect; he could not reconcile his tremendous speed and preference for making the running with staying the Derby distance. "To be on him was like riding a creature that combined the power of an elephant with the speed of a greyhound."

Atty Persse recorded his own observations on The Tetrarch as an individual: "His development in every respect was abnormal. He was a very strong shouldered horse, possessed of a tremendous long rein, with a wonderful hind leg which gave him that remarkable leverage. Indeed his development behind the saddle was phenomenal. He had that almost straight, powerful hind leg which all good horses have, pronounced second thighs, was very high and truly moulded over the loins and had a beautiful intelligent head. He was slightly dipped in his back (this dip became very pronounced in old age). His action was remarkable. When he galloped his back seemed to get shorter and his legs longer."

From a trainer's viewpoint The Tetrarch had two great

attributes: he was a good worker on the home gallops so one always knew the time of day with him, and he was also a great doer. "I think a great many races are won in a horse's manger," Atty Persse observed. "One of the heartiest grubbers I ever handled was The Tetrarch. He always ate 21lbs of oats (per day) and never left a grain."

The grey was a great character too. Normally amenable in and out of the stable, he could be intractable when so inclined. He had a couple of traits that he shared with another outstanding racehorse and sire in Hyperion – he hated having a physic ball with the taste of bitter aloes, and on occasions he would come to a halt at exercise and stare into the distance until such time as he felt inclined to move. He also had a strong aversion to being shod by a stranger, particularly with any onlookers, and, after his début, the Chattis Hill farrier always accompanied him to race-meetings.

A more serious flaw for a potential stallion was that he exhibited a marked lack of sexual libido. Dermot McCalmont described The Tetrarch's attitude to sex as "monastic in the extreme". It took all the patience and perseverance of the staff at his owner's Ballylinch Stud to persuade him to cover any mares at all despite both the expertise at hand and the up-to-date facilities. Furthermore his performance in the covering yard often masked the fact that he had failed to ejaculate.

In charge was the newly appointed stud groom, Harry Sharpe. A man whose enormous experience had been gained at William Hall-Walker's stud at Tully, now the Irish National Stud, he was already the author of *The Practical Stud Groom* which became a standard reference book on the subject. Another bonus at Ballylinch was a new indoor covering yard, one of the first of its kind, if not the first, in the British Isles.

The horse started off at a fee of 300 guineas, rising to 500 guineas. Because of his reluctance to cover (all work on the stud had to cease as even the sound of someone hammering in the distance was sufficient to distract him from the job in hand), the grey proved a dismal foal-getter and his record became progressively worse with the passing of the years; he had been sterile for ten years before his death in August 1935 aged twenty-four.

The Tetrarch is buried at Ballylinch, as are his son, Tetratema, together with the latter's son, Mr. Jinks. From 1916 to 1926 he sired just 130 live foals of which eighty were winners in Great Britain and Ireland. In the circumstances he did remarkably well to be champion sire in 1919 and to finish third on the list in both 1920 and 1923.

His achievement in siring three winners of the St. Leger in Caligula, a grey, Polemarch and Salmon-Trout, within the space of five years, lends support to the view that he might have stayed sufficiently well to win a classic, but conversely the fact that his long-term influence was transmitted to subsequent generations by his grey offspring, Tetratema and Mumtaz Mahal, both major influences for speed, makes it all a matter of sheer conjecture.

In his dotage when he went completely white, The Tetrarch's daily routine involved being ridden down to deliver and collect the mail from the local post office. But for the twin misfortunes of injury and infertility, this particular postman would probably have been regarded as the greatest horse since St. Simon.

It is inevitable that a horse of The Tetrarch's standing would have a race named after him and he is commemorated in Ireland, the land of his birth where he also spent the duration of his stud life, by the Group 3 The Tetrarch Stakes at the Curragh, a trial over 7 furlongs for the Irish Two Thousand Guineas.

Less predictable is his memorial in Stockbridge. Not many racehorses receive official recognition from on high, but over the archway leading to the choir vestry in St. Peter's Church in the High Street are a pair of small roundels painted by Lionel Edwards. The one on the left-hand depicts a brace of trout from the River Test and on the right is the unmistakable head of The Tetrarch.

Lynwood Palmer was yet another famous equine artist to paint The Tetrarch, but this was a portrait with a difference as

Dermot McCalmont commissioned two separate pictures simultaneously – one of his near-side and one of his off-side, the reason being that the markings were so dissimilar. Dermot and Atty each had a painting, the original intention being that when one of them died his painting would pass to the survivor. However, when the trainer died aged ninety-one in 1960 (the owner died eight years later), he bequeathed his painting to The Queen and it found a new home in the Royal Box at Ascot.

Thoroughbred lineage frequently hangs by the narrowest of threads and that is certainly true of The Tetrarch. When he was a foal, John Peard of Woodpark Stud, Co. Meath (where *Grey Magic* star Caterina was bred), was on the verge of buying the impressive grey colt with the distinctive markings for £800. But on being told that the intention was to, "Cut him and put him by to make a jumper," the breeder, Cub Kennedy, retorted, "In that case I won't sell him to you and the deal is off."

In this haphazard way an irrevocable disaster for the future of the breed was averted. Certainly without the patriarchal figure of the Spotted Wonder, *Grey Magic* would never have come to be written.

TOWN CRIER

Grey, 1965, by Sovereign Path - Corsley Bell

Owner: Sir Evelyn de Rothschild
Trainer: Peter Walwyn
Jockey: Duncan Keith
Breeder: Southcourt Stud

What do Absalom, Colonist II, Saritamer and Town Crier have in common? Answer: all are greys who stood for part of their stallion careers in England at Southcourt Stud, near Leighton Buzzard, in Bedfordshire, just down the railway line from Cheddington, where the Great Train Robbery took place.

Town Crier was bred and foaled at Southcourt Stud, which is managed by Renée Robeson, and he raced in the colours of her brother, Sir Evelyn de Rothschild, former chairman of N.M. Rothschild and now head of the family investment bank.

The Rothschilds acquired Southcourt Stud in about 1870 and it is in the same vicinity as two other Rothschild studs which also produced noted greys in the post-war period, the now defunct Mentmore, where the 6th Lord Rosebery bred his Oaks winner, Sleeping Partner, and Waddesdon, where Dorothy de Rothschild bred Scallywag – a useful jumping sire, he was such a large framed individual that he had the greatest difficulty fitting into the starting stalls.

Obviously it was very rewarding for Mrs. Robeson and her husband, Peter, who made his name riding the celebrated Craven A in international show jumping events, to have a home-bred horse with Town Crier's credentials standing at Southcourt.

Along with three other greys featured in *Grey Magic*, Habat, Humble Duty and Pasty, he was trained by Peter Walwyn in Lambourn; like Humble Duty he was by Sovereign Path.

Renée Robeson remembers that Peter Walwyn was not that enamoured with Town Crier when he first saw him as a yearling at Southcourt, "The colt was on the small side and he much preferred another grey, who looked to have infinitely more scope." But handsome is as handsome does and it was Town Crier who delivered the goods.

A colt who improved throughout his career, Town Crier seemed to have a particular liking for Ascot where he won the Queen Anne Stakes (beating his subsequent stud companion, Jimmy Reppin), as well as the Victoria Cup as a four-year-old – at the previous year's Royal Meeting he was runner-up in the Jersey Stakes; he was also third twice in the Hungerford Stakes at Newbury.

Over the years Rénee Robeson, a licensed trainer at Newport Pagnell, had a long association with the old British Bloodstock Agency and the horse stood under their management at Southcourt, one of the principal attractions being that he was by an acknowledged sire of sires in Sovereign Path from whom he inherited his colour.

From only his second crop of foals Town Crier sired the brilliant grey, Cry of Truth, who was the champion two-year-old filly of 1974. Another of his offspring, Town And Country, was destined to make a significant impact as a British-based National Hunt sire – he was bred by Tom Egerton at Chaddleworth, near Newbury, where his son, Charlie, now trains.

VIGO

Grey, 1953, by Vilmorin - Thomasina

Owner: Thomas Farr
Trainer: Bill Dutton
Jockey: Lester Piggott
Breeder: Thomas Farr

Three homebred colts provided Thomas Farr of Ruddington Grange in Nottinghamshire with a memorable year in 1957, the sprinter Vigo (July Cup), the miler Quorum (Sussex Stakes), and the stayer, Sandiacre (Cesarewitch); Vigo and Sandiacre were trained by Bill Dutton, a solicitor by profession, at Malton in Yorkshire.

Not only were Vigo and Quorum greys, but they were also closely related as they were sons of Vilmorin and the progeny of half-sisters, Thomasina and Akimbo respectively. Furthermore at that time Bill Dutton's Grove Cottage Stables also housed another grey winner of the July Cup in Right Boy.

Successful five times as a juvenile when ridden exclusively by freelance light-weight jockey, Jack Brace, Vigo had finished third that season in the National Breeders' Produce Stakes behind Rustam and Palariva. It was to the smart French-trained grey filly, Palariva, that Vigo was runner-up as a three-year-old, beaten a short head, in the King's Stand Stakes, and third in the King George Stakes.

By now Lester Piggott was Vigo's regular partner and they teamed up the following season to win the July Cup by three lengths from Drum Beat to whom he was conceding a stone;

subsequently they finished third to Gratitude and stable-companion, Right Boy, in the Nunthorpe Stakes. This was a vintage collection of sprinters that also included Ennis and Matador.

Vigo was syndicated to cover his first mares in 1958 at Archie McIntyre's Theakston Stud, near Bedale in Yorkshire, which became famous for breeding another celebrated grey at about the same time in Sovereign Path. He remained there for five seasons, during which time he sired a number of smart sprinters, before being sold to Cranagh Castle Stud in Ireland.

Cranagh Castle, Templemore, Co. Tipperary, was owned by Ted Corbett, who in conjunction with the British Bloodstock Agency, opened up the bloodstock market to Japan (despite having been a Japanese prisoner of war), and soon Vigo was winging his way to the Far East. Ted Corbett's son, John, founded London-based Heron Bloodstock Services, once a leading international bloodstock agency.

It was wonderful for the Yorkshireman when, in 2005, home-bred La Cucaracha provided Guy Reed with his first ever Group 1 Victory, in the Nunthorpe Stakes.

VILMORIN

Grey, 1943, by Gold Bridge - Queen of the Meadows

Owner: John Read
Trainers: Joe Lawson, Norman Scobie
Jockey: Cliff Richards
Breeder: The Hon. George Lambton

There was a sensational finish to the 1946 King's Stand Stakes, which concluded the substitute Royal Meeting at Ascot (during the war it was designated a Heath Meeting) with three-year-old Vilmorin, ridden by Gordon Richards' younger brother, Cliff, defeating his elders, Golden Cloud (another son of Gold Bridge), and Royal Charger by two short heads. All three horses were destined to become singularly influential sires.

A dapple grey, Vilmorin was bred by the Newmarket trainer, George Lambton, and he had trained Golden Cloud until his death in July 1945 whereupon his son, Teddy, took over the responsibility for his mother's good sprinter. Vilmorin was then trained at Manton by Joe Lawson for John Read, a farmer from Downton in Wiltshire. He had paid 510 guineas for the colt as a yearling at the Newmarket September Sales and put him in training with Norman Scobie at Whitsbury, near Fordingbridge, in Hampshire.

Vilmorin soon proved well bought, winning four of his five juvenile starts. In April, on his début at Salisbury his local course, he scored at 25-1 to land a tremendous off-course gamble. But as William Hill, the great bookmaker and owner of Whitsbury, had failed to execute the stable commission as instructed, landlord and tenant became embroiled in bitter litigation. Norman Scobie sued for slander in the High Court, but lost the case.

Shortly after his Royal Ascot victory Vilmorin suffered a fetlock injury and was retired to stand at Stackallen Stud, Co. Meath, but his owner then repatriated him to his own Redenham Park Stud, Weyhill, near Andover. Nowadays Redenham Park is where Bridget Swire, the principal patron of Jonathan Geake's local Kimpton Down Stables, boards her mares.

Subsequently Vilmorin was moved to Littleton Stud, outside Winchester, owned by Gerald Deane, one-time senior partner in Tattersalls – later his son, Bruce, also a Tattersalls' director, would stand Vilmorin's grey son, Quorum (sire of Red Rum) there. Nowadays Littleton is owned by Jeff Smith, whose colours are synonymous with Lochsong and Persian Punch.

By the time of his death aged twenty in August 1963, Vilmorin had earned a considerable reputation as a sire whose stock were noted for their soundness and good temperaments. While Quorum was a miler, most of the others were sprinters, amongst them the July Cup winners, Vigo and Vilmoray, as well as Chris (King's Stand Stakes), and Gay Mairi (Nunthorpe Stakes). Both Vigo and Chris were Yorkshire-trained greys.

Vilmorin's greatest influence in the long-term has been as a sire of broodmares. Two noteworthy greys were Jojo, dam of Queen's Hussar, and the Wigans' celebrated foundation mare, Pelting. Another grey daughter, Intent, is the dam of top sprinter, Song, Quorum's successor at Littleton Stud.

WARPATH

Grey, 1969, by Sovereign Path - Ardneasken

Owner: Guy Reed
Trainer: Sam Hall
Jockey: Alec Russell
Breeder: Guy Reed

At one time Guy Reed, now a leading patron of Barry Hills' Lambourn stable, was the biggest owner-breeder north of the Trent and the whole enterprise revolved around his homebred grey stallion, Warpath.

The odyssey began with the purchase of the mare, Ardneasken, from David Wills' Hadrian Stud at the 1968 Newmarket December Sales for 14,000 guineas with Warpath 'in utero'. With a son worthy to stand at stud here and additional winners of the calibre of Dakota, who also carried Guy Reed's striking colours 'gold and black checks, pink sleeves and cap', with distinction, Ardneasken became a noteworthy foundation mare.

Guy Reed, a Yorkshireman born and bred, owned two studs within striking distance of Harrogate, Nidd Hall at Ripley and Copgrove Hall at Burton Leonard. In addition he also became the owner of Spigot Lodge Stables in Middleham, presided over by Sam Hall, another Yorkshireman. It was at Nidd Hall that Warpath spent his entire stud career.

Warpath had strong pedigree links with Yorkshire too. His sire, Sovereign Path, was bred at Theakston Stud, Bedale, and his dam, Ardneasken, was a half-sister to Cash And Courage, a good horse trained by Sam Hall. Coincidentally, they belong to the family of Lost Soul, the foundation mare of the greatest Yorkshire breeder of his time; Lionel Holliday, he used to own Copgrove Hall which he ran in conjunction with his celebrated Cleaboy Stud in Ireland.

Winner of the Doonside Cup at the Ayr Western Meeting and valuable 10 furlong handicaps at Goodwood and Newcastle as a three-year-old, Warpath was destined to make a far greater impact as a stallion than he had done on the racecourse, thanks almost entirely to Guy Reed's considerable private broodmare band.

The most distinguished of Warpath's progeny trained at Spigot Lodge (where Chris Thornton succeeded Sam Hall), was the grey, Shotgun, who carried Guy Reed's colours into fourth place in Shergar's Derby. As his offspring were invariably tough and genuine, he also made a very marked contribution with his runners under National Hunt Rules and his grey son, Celio Rufo, helped to maintain the status quo in Ireland.

Warpath had a superior younger half-brother in Dakota. Successful in the St. Simon Stakes and Ebor Handicap and fourth in the King George VI and Queen Elizabeth Stakes, this near-black colt, who had a questionable temperament and was invariably equipped with blinkers, was sold to the Polish National Stud where he became a champion sire.

Guy Reed has a direct link with Galen Weston Snr, breeder of another star of *Grey Magic* in Bruni. A partner with his brother in Allied Farm Foods, they sold the business to Weston's Associated British Foods. The merry-go-round continued when ABF eventually became part of Hillsdown Holdings, a food orientated company started by David Thompson of Cheveley Park Stud.

WHAT'S UP BOYS

Grey, 1994, by Supreme Leader - Maryville Bick

Owner: R.J.B. Partners
Trainer: Philip Hobbs
Jockeys: Richard Johnson, Paul Flynn
Breeder: David Cahill

It is astonishing that the three big West Country trainers who dominate National Hunt racing to such an extent, have all gained significant success with greys; Martin Pipe with Baron Blakeney in the Triumph Hurdle; Paul Nicholls with Call Equiname in the Queen Mother Champion 'Chase; and Philip Hobbs with What's Up Boys in the Hennessy Cognac Gold Cup.

In forty-five runnings of the Hennessy, Newbury's premier steeplechase, What's Up Boys became the fifth grey to prevail. Stalbridge Colonist won a memorable contest at the expense of Arkle way back in 1966, but the 1990s produced three winners in quick succession with One Man, Suny Bay and Teeton Mill, all celebrities featured in *Grey Magic*.

When What's Up Boys won at Newbury by a neck after a thrilling tussle with the ill-fated Behrajan, he was just seven years old yet he never won another race. Up till then Philip Hobbs had regarded him as a spring horse who appreciated top of the ground, but his victory on soft ground at Newbury on the first day of December called for a reappraisal.

He may not have won again, but he did put up three noteworthy performances that season, finishing fourth in the Welsh National to Supreme Glory, fifth to Best Mate on the first of the latter's three Cheltenham Gold Cup triumphs, and runner-up in the Grand National to Bindaree.

Having made significant progress on the second circuit at Aintree, he jumped the last upsides Bindaree and forged clear only to lose the advantage in the shadow of the post, beaten one and three-quarter lengths. Had he prevailed it would have been only the fourth time that a grey had won the world's most famous steeplechase and the only grey to do so equipped with blinkers. It was a gallant effort as he was conceding weight to all but three of his thirty-nine rivals.

At the previous year's Grand National meeting, What's Up Boys had won the Grade 2 Mildmay Novices' 'Chase before finishing runner-up in the Whitbread Gold Cup, a tremendous effort for one with such limited experience over fences. Initially an inept jumper, he developed into a top novice hurdler, winning the Grade 2 Winter Novices' Hurdle, Sandown Park, the Coral Cup at the Cheltenham festival and the Champion Novice Hurdle, Punchestown.

In December 2004, it was announced that the grey son of Supreme Leader would be retired. Paying tribute to his former charge whom he originally bought in Ireland, Philip Hobbs, commented, "How many horses won at three festivals as well as winning a Hennessy and finishing second in the Grand National? He had a pretty amazing record and was a lovely horse to deal with."

By then What's Up Boys was owned by Jacky Deithrick, who had inherited the gelding upon the death of her father, Dr. Roden Bridgewater. She had transferred the 10-year-old to Henrietta Knight's stable in the hope that a change of scenery might rekindle his enthusiasm, but it was not to be and he was retired to her farm in north Cornwall.

YOUNG EMPEROR

Grey, 1963, by Grey Sovereign - Young Empress

Owner: Pansy Parker Poe
Trainer: Paddy Prendergast Snr.
Jockey: Lester Piggott
Breeder: Pansy Parker Poe

From his powerful stables at Maddenstown on the Curragh, Paddy Prendergast Snr. plundered many top prizes in England during the 1950s and 1960s; indeed he was the leading trainer here for three consecutive years from 1963 to 1965.

This provided a remarkable comeback for the Irish maestro as he had been warned off over the running of the two-year-old, Blue Sail, when favourite for the Cornwallis Stakes at Ascot in the autumn of 1953. In finishing second, beaten a neck, the stewards of the Jockey Club maintained that the colt's performance 'was inconsistent with his previous running in Ireland.'

To emphasise the controversy surrounding that decision, the equivalent Irish Turf authorities did not impose a corresponding ban which would have been the normal practice. When his licence was reinstated in August 1954, the Irishman celebrated his return with four winners at the York Ebor Meeting. Acknowledged as one of the best yearling judges in the business, he was also one of the first trainers to introduce interval training, and soon he had established an unrivalled record with two-year-olds.

Amongst them were no fewer than six winners of the Coventry Stakes and four winners of the Gimcrack Stakes. Two of them proceeded to win both races, The Pie King and Pansy Parker

Poe's Young Emperor. Regarded by his trainer as the fastest of them all, the son of Grey Sovereign won at Royal Ascot by six lengths and at York by seven lengths (from another grey Grey Sovereign colt in Lanark), to earn top ranking on the Free Handicap.

His third victory from four starts, Young Emperor was equipped with blinkers in the Gimcrack in an attempt to avoid a repetition of his surly behaviour at Goodwood. As a son of Grey Sovereign he could be temperamental and before the Richmond Stakes he had refused to line up with his only two opponents at the old fashioned barrier – the judge stayed in his box sufficiently long to accord the grey third place when he eventually condescended to canter past the winning post.

That season Pansy Parker Poe became the leading breeder in Great Britain and Ireland as, in addition to Young Emperor, she was also responsible for Meadow Court. Likewise trained by Paddy Prendergast, he won the Irish (Sweeps) Derby and the King George VI and Queen Elizabeth Stakes. Both colts were Irish-bred – their breeder boarded a handful of mares at Kildangan Stud, albeit she had her own stud, Shawnee Farm, in her native USA.

Unlike his dam, Young Empress, who was beaten a short head for the Irish One Thousand Guineas and whose half-brother, Nagami (by Grey Sovereign's three-parts brother, Nimbus), was placed in all three Triple Crown events, Young Emperor did not train on as a three-year-old. That season he was sold for stallion duties in the 'States. In due course he followed Nagami to Italy after an interim period standing at Old Connell Stud, Co. Kildare, in Ireland.

One of Young Emperor's best known representatives in the UK was the grey Dragonara Palace – the achievements of this American-bred have already been chronicled in earlier pages.

INDEX OF PEOPLE

INDEX OF PEOPLE

INDEX OF HORSES

251

INDEX OF RACEHORSES

INDEX OF RACEHORSES

PHOTOGRAPHIC ACKNOWLEDGMENTS

Plate 1 : *Top: Mirrorpix/Martin Lynch; middle and bottom: Rouch Wilmot Library*

Plate 2: *Top: Racing Post/Ed Whitaker; bottom: George Selwyn.*

Plate 3: *Top: Press Association; bottom: Rouch Wilmot Library*

Plate 4: *Top and bottom: Rouch Wilmot Library; middle: Mirrorpix*

Plate 5: *Top: Rouch Wilmot Library*

Plate 6: *Main picture: Racing Post/Ed Whitaker;*

Plate 7: *Top: Gerry Cranham; bottom: Rouch Wilmot Library*

Plate 8 : *All photographs: Rouch Wilmot Library*